BASICS

FASHION DESIGN

07

MENSWEAR

Ethical: awareness/ reflection/ debate

An AVA Book
Published by AVA Publishing SA
Rue des Fontenailles 16
Case Postale
1000 Lausanne 6
Switzerland
Tel: +41 786 005 109
Email: enquiries@avabooks.com

Distributed by Thames & Hudson (ex-North America)
181a High Holborn
London WC1V 7QX
United Kingdom
Tel: +44 20 7845 5000
Fax: +44 20 7845 5055
Email: sales@thameshudson.co.uk
www.thamesandhudson.com

Distributed in the USA & Canada by:
Ingram Publisher Services Inc.
1 Ingram Blvd.
La Vergne TN 37086
USA
Tel: +1 866 400 5351
Fax: +1 800 838 1149
Email: customer.service@ingrampublisherservices.com

English Language Support Office
AVA Publishing (UK) Ltd.
Tel: +44 1903 204 455
Email: enquiries@avabooks.com

ISBN 978-2-940411-43-6

Library of Congress Cataloging-in-Publication Data
Hopkins, John.
Basics Fashion Design 07: Menswear /John Hopkins p. cm.
Includes bibliographical references and index.
ISBN: 9782940411436 (pbk.:alk.paper)
eISBN: 9782940447145
1.Men's clothing industry--Study and teaching.
2.Fashion design--Study and teaching.
3.Design--Study and teaching.
TT580 .H665 2011

10 9 8 7 6 5 4 3 2 1

Design by John F McGill.

Production by AVA Book Production Pte. Ltd., Singapore
Tel: +65 6334 8173
Fax: +65 6259 9830
Email: production@avabooks.com.sg

Line-up of male models in a simulated 1950s office space presented by American menswear designer Thom Browne at Pitti Uomo fair in Florence, Italy.

Contents

Basics Fashion Design: Menswear offers a visually engaging and fresh perspective on this fascinating and subtly complex area of fashion. It examines the historical and social evolution of menswear through the ages and the influence of court and mercantile dress styles, uniforms and military dress. It considers the rich history and traditions of men's tailoring, comparing and contrasting the sartorial traditions of London's Savile Row and the 'British look' with the equally distinctive soft tailoring traditions from Italy and the all-American preppy look. Men's sportswear, and the unparalleled impact of denim, are also considered as part of the story. The final part of the book examines design processes for menswear; how themes, concepts and influences can be translated into credible sources of research for menswear design.

With a variety of inspirational imagery and insightful contributions from menswear specialists, this book is intended to stimulate your interest in this fascinating area of fashion and to enhance your appreciation for the many technologies and traditions that have their roots in menswear design.

The Burberry menswear A/W10 collection had heavy military influences.

'Clothes make the man. Naked people have little or no influence on society.'
Mark Twain

It is only the modern that ever becomes old-fashioned.

Oscar Wilde

The history of menswear is also the history of human dress throughout the ages. It is a fascinating and complex journey through distinct social and cultural contexts.

This chapter offers an introduction to the historical and social evolution of menswear, which considers the role and influence of court and mercantile dress styles, uniforms and military dress. Menswear's influence on womenswear is considered, as well as the sway of male style icons and their role in defining and redefining an 'ideal' or standard within the social and increasingly media-orientated contexts of music, film and sport.

The ancient world

- Draped styles predominate for men and women
- Dyeing and pleating techniques develop
- Greek civilization establishes classical proportions
- Woollen and linen fabrics are widely used
- Roman dress styles for men reinforce status and class

The middle ages

- Barbarian men favour loose-fitting tunics worn with stockings (called hose)
- European society organizes itself into royal courts, which set court dress styles
- Tunic styles evolve into more complex forms with shaping and decoration added
- Trade and craft skills organized into guilds
- Men's clothing styles regulated by sumptuary laws to assert class and status
- Fur widely worn by nobility
- Hoods, capes and layers of tunics are commonly worn
- Increased tendency towards cutting and shaping men's clothes
- The cotehardie, a long tunic style, evolves into a shortened jacket
- Hanging sleeve fashion predominates
- Lavish Burgundian courts influence clothing styles in Europe
- Increased use of silks

The Renaissance

- Clothing styles for men evolve into northern European and regional Italian variations
- Fashion for slashing (panes) and a broader silhouette are popular in northern Europe
- Men's doublet styles worn with form-fitting hose
- Jerkin styles are introduced
- Padding and quilting techniques develop and influence the silhouette
- Men's hose style develops into upper padded trunk hose and nether hose (stockings)
- Doublet styles with a peascod belly are popular for men
- Goffered (pleated) frill on undershirts evolve into neck ruffs for men
- Spanish court style popularizes the wearing of black
- Starch introduced to stiffen clothing
- Looser-fitting Venetian breeches and slops replace padded trunk hose

⮝⮝⮝ Detail of a 15th century illuminated manuscript shows men wearing tunics and hose.

⮝⮝ Albrecht Dürer self-portrait of 1498. He wears elegant, aristocratic clothing to show off his social standing.

⮝ Baroque painting by Spanish artist Diego Velázquez, in which the subject wears a ruff collar.

Baroque

- Ribbons and lace become popular for men and women
- Lace collars become highly fashionable
- The cavalier style predominates for men during early Baroque period
- Puritan style favours black clothing without decoration
- Leather boots with spurs become fashionable
- French court becomes the most influential in Europe, setting men's fashion styles
- French and English courts introduce a longer fitting cassock/casaque coat style, worn with a waistcoat that replaces the doublet
- Wigs become fashionable for men
- Petticoat breeches worn by fashionable men
- Tricorne hats and buckled shoes are widely worn
- The cassock coat evolves into a justacorps style: a knee-length coat fitted to the waist

Rococo to Revolution

- Cotton mills established in France and England to meet popular demand for cotton fabrics
- Knee-length breeches cut closer to the body with a front 'fall' opening for men
- Men's wig fashion reaches its zenith
- Greatcoat and frock coat styles introduced for men in England
- The English riding habit style becomes fashionable
- Stand-fall collars developed on men's coats
- Sumptuary laws repealed in France as part of the French Revolution
- Loose-fitting bridge trousers, based on English sailor pants, are introduced by French revolutionaries to replace knee breeches, which are associated with bourgeois styles
- Knee-length breeches and wigs quickly go out of fashion

Empire to Romantic

- There are more variations on the English riding habit
- Double-breasted tailcoat style and pantaloons are introduced
- Cropped Spencer jacket is introduced
- Stovepipe hat style evolves into the top hat
- Neck cravats (stocks) become essential dress for gentlemen
- Beau Brummell adapts English country styles to the gentleman's wardrobe and establishes accepted standards for male grooming

19th century

- Men's dress styles are increasingly dominated by sober colours including black, navy and greys
- Body belts (the male corset) and thigh padding are briefly introduced around the 1830s as part of a more rounded, tailored silhouette
- Frock coats, riding coats and pantaloons continue to be worn
- Gigot sleeves are introduced on men's coats
- Foundation of Savile Row in London advances tailoring techniques
- Black-tie and white-tie protocols established for men's formal attire
- Sack jacket (also known as a lounge jacket) is introduced as daywear
- The riding coat evolves into a morning coat
- The reefer coat style is introduced
- The four-in-hand neck tie dressing introduced
- Sewing machines are introduced and increase capability for the manufacture and production of men's clothing
- English sporting styles continue to evolve with the introduction of tweed jackets in Norfolk style and sack jackets cut in sporting tweeds
- The Chesterfield topcoat introduced
- Jersey 'combination' undergarments are worn

◆◆◆ Tricorne hats were widely worn during the Baroque period.

◆◆ Felipe I, Duke of Parma, wears Spanish court dress in this 18th-century portrait by Laurent Pécheux.

◆ Black formal dressing for men was established by the early 19th century.

20th century

- Sack jackets are worn with matching trousers as the basis of the working suit
- Trouser creases are introduced for menswear during the first decade
- Formal attire established during the 19th century remains in force with only minor variations. Spats or gaiters are sometimes added
- Driving and duster coat styles developed for men as car driving becomes popular
- The military trench coat style is adapted to civilian dress
- Boxer shorts are introduced as men's undergarments
- European and American styles of men's tailoring develop their own identities
- Fashionable preferences move between single-breasted and double-breasted suits and jackets, with variations on shoulder cuts and lapel styling.
- Ready-to-wear and 'off the peg' clothing becomes more readily available to male consumers
- Rapid advances in sports fabrics are developed for easier washing and wearing properties
- The growing influence of youth cultures popularizes denim jeans and casual sports styles
- Ski wear, active sports and textile technologies advance sportswear styles for men
- Popular music and media influences expand the boundaries of male dress for daywear and leisure
- Menswear design labels establish strong market presence alongside more established practices of bespoke clothing, such as Savile Row
- Advancing technologies in textiles and media communications continue to expand and evolve modern menswear

For the purposes of this chapter we will begin by distinguishing between the notion of male dress and 'fashionable' male dress, since the latter is generally applied to the courtly system of dressing, which was established around the late middle ages. Essentially, two main forms of male dress emerged. The first was the draped style of dress for men. Draped styles were characterized by the arrangement of large pieces of rectangular, oval or crescent-shaped fabric, which we commonly associate with the ancient Greeks, Romans or Etruscans. These fabric lengths were folded, pinned, pleated or belted around the body in different ways. This early style of dressing utilized all the fabric that was woven, ensuring there was no waste.

The second form of dress, which was essential to the development of menswear, was the 'shaped' or 'tailored' style. Although this approach to dressing is generally attributed to a later evolution of men's clothing, its origins may even go back to man's earliest attempts to shape animal skins to parts of the human body. The different sizes, textures and shapes of the skins would necessitate a different approach to their use and function when applied to cover or adorn the human figure. The evolution of draped and early tailored styles varied according to the available or local resources and technologies of a particular geographic region, taking into account differences in local customs and practices.

Sporting costumes for men from French fashion plate, July 1880.

O The Greek himation robe, as shown on this statue of the Greek philosopher Sophocles, represented status; it was worn by men in the upper classes.

Function and status

The most defining characteristics of male dress are determined by a man's function and status, which have had a huge impact on the development of menswear and styles of dress. Clothing serves both a practical purpose and an aesthetic role. One of the underlying principles that has defined menswear through the ages is that of dressing to communicate who we are, in terms of gender, social status and culture.

The early men's dress styles that we commonly associate with the ancient Greeks and Romans appear at first to be almost indistinguishable; however, there are many subtle and significant differences between them. The drapes, folds and pleat formations on male Greek dress were generally the more artistic and aesthetic of the two; the Greeks had a relaxed approach to nudity and the male body. A man's status was recognized by his wearing an enveloping himation robe or a male chiton tunic; the shorter exomis tunics were worn by lower-class men and slaves. The arrangement of hair, including facial hair, was another important signifier of a man's status and position in society.

O Statue of Augustus as Pontifex Maximus wearing the toga.

The development of Roman men's dress was influenced by the Etruscans. It was more class-based and codified than that of the ancient Greeks and reflected Roman society's formal distinctions between its own citizens and outsiders, in what was a highly organized system of rule and governance. The Roman toga has come to embody this more than any other garment of the ancient world. The strict rules of dress were determined by a man's patrician (social) status and rank, up to and including the emperor. The toga's overall colour, its border (called a *praetexta*) and its fabric all conveyed meaning. Consequently, the Roman toga evolved into an item of ceremonial dress.

Sumptuary laws

One of the more interesting aspects of menswear through the ages is the pervasive influence and impact of sumptuary laws. Essentially, these laws prescribed and reinforced social hierarchies and perceived morals through restrictions on clothing, decoration and luxury expenditure. The introduction of sumptuary laws in the middle ages, and their relatively widespread use until the 17th century, became a means of maintaining and reinforcing class distinctions and wealth.

Dress regulation was a feature of life during Roman times, perhaps most notably the restricted use of Tyrian (royal) purple. This effectively rendered purple-dyed textiles as status symbols, with use restricted and reserved for high-ranking Romans and the Emperor himself. These laws persisted throughout the Byzantine Empire, when the state controlled the price and quantity of imported goods and regulated domestic manufacturing through the establishment of guilds. With the introduction of silk weaving in Europe around AD 550, silk production became a state-owned monopoly and its use limited to garments and lavish embroideries for the wealthiest citizens as well as courtiers and high priests.

Sumptuary laws remained a consistent feature of Tudor England under King Henry VIII, who set the dress standard for his royal court. He had an imposing presence, and aspirations to compete with the two main European powers of the day, France and the Holy Roman Empire. This famously culminated in the so-called 'Field of Cloth of Gold' meeting between Henry and Francis I of France in 1520, which amounted to little more than an ostentatious display of wealth. Later, in 1574, Queen Elizabeth I of England introduced a series of sumptuary laws, which included for men the banning of 'any silk of the colour of purple, cloth of gold tissued, nor fur of sables, but only the King, Queen, King's mother, children, brethren, and sisters, uncles and aunts; and except dukes, marquises, and earls, who may wear the same in doublets, jerkins, linings of cloaks, gowns, and hose; and those of the Garter, purple in mantles only.' The rules of dressing remained a priority for the royal courts of Europe and were upheld through the system of guilds.

◐ This portrait of King Henry VIII emphasizes the broad, layered silhouette and decorative slashes of male dress of the northern Renaissance.

Courtly dressing

Although courtly dressing can be traced back to the civilizations of the ancient world, most notably the dynastic kingdoms of the Ancient Egyptian Pharaohs, it was not until the middle ages that the word 'fashion' could be used to describe this collective style. During these times, the fashionable style of dress in Europe was set by the royal courts, each with a monarch and a hierarchy of nobility in attendance. Increasingly, being 'fashionable' meant dressing and behaving in order to express one's social class and dignity.

In the male-dominated societies of the middle ages, men's fashionable dress was characterized by the use of lavish fabrics, vivid colours and ostentatious detailing. European textile workers became more skilled in producing refined silks and brocades that had previously been imported from the East. This period also witnessed the development of more form-fitting men's clothes that were cut to fit around the body and emphasize the male torso.

During the 15th century, men's dress styles of Northern Europe were greatly influenced by the most lavish and fashionable court of the period, Burgundy. Even the demise of Burgundian power in 1477 influenced male dress when Swiss soldiers and German mercenaries on the battlefield were amazed by the lavish textiles and set about cutting them up and inserting them through their own clothes by pulling them through slashed openings. This gave rise to a court fashion that was prevalent during the reign of King Henry VIII of England.

The structures and protocols of opulent court dressing remained a feature of male dress during subsequent centuries. The 16th century marked the rise of Spanish court styles and the introduction of 'severe black' for men, which was offset by a striking white neck ruff. Later, as France became Europe's pre-eminent power, the lavish court dress styles of King Louis XIV were widely exported across Europe to other courts.

The French Revolution of the late 18th century interrupted this established court system of defining fashionable men's dress: the clothing and textile guilds were abolished and France's sumptuary laws were repealed. Napoleon Bonaparte later revived a classically inspired court system but by this time European courts competed for influence and courtly male dress became more ceremonial, inspired by military associations.

Elaborate, stiffened materials were worn by 16th-century noblemen including this example of a cape coat worn over a doublet and padded hose.

Icon: Edward, Prince of Wales

Also known as the Duke of Windsor and briefly King Edward VIII before his abdication in 1936 to marry Wallis Simpson, Edward was a menswear trend setter during his early life. As Prince of Wales, his personal style and impeccable taste made him a style icon. He popularized the wearing of plus-four trousers for playing golf and the check pattern that carries the name Prince of Wales, making it acceptable attire for men's lounge suits.

'Let it not be assumed that clothes have ever been a fetish of mine. Rather have I become, by force of circumstances and upbringing, clothes-conscious. My position as Prince of Wales dictated that I should always be well and suitably dressed for every conceivable occasion.'
Edward VIII

Mercantile dress

Mercantile dress, an established mode of dress worn by the merchant or commercial classes, evolved outside the rigours of the court system. It became increasingly relevant in the 18th and 19th centuries, with the start of the Industrial Revolution and the growth of a well-defined middle-class population in Europe and North America.

The French Revolution in the late 18th century had a profound effect on men's dress styles, which is still evident today. One of its biggest impacts was the move away from ostentatious modes of dress, lavish decoration and flamboyant use of colour. The Revolution's so-called 'reign of terror' meant that it became very dangerous to wear flamboyant, 'fashionable' clothes and a move towards simplicity and the abandonment of decoration became inevitable. English sailor pants were adopted as a new style for men and quickly became a political symbol of revolt as these styles represented the common working man. The period also marked the beginning of a more austere dress code for men, with blues, blacks and browns as the prevailing colour palette. Moreover, in keeping with the social mood of the period, men were encouraged to turn towards more 'serious' matters than those implied by dressing up. Menswear accordingly adopted an air of restraint and sobriety in the new, rapidly industrializing society.

19th-century portrait of a gentleman, by George Clint.

In 19th-century England, menswear was increasingly influenced by 'country living' styles, which originated from the landed gentry and reflected their interests in rural activities such as horse riding and hunting. Men's outfits were usually accented by details such as leather riding boots and kid gloves. Many tailored styles were introduced, including the redingote or 'riding coat', the tailcoat and the frock coat, as well as crisp high collars and cravats, all of which have since evolved into the staple pieces of a man's wardrobe.

The early manifestations of military dress were concerned with the practical nature of warfare. This gave rise to several distinct forms of armour, which included mail or chain-mail, a form of armour constructed of multiple interlocking metal rings that were shaped into a mail shirt or hauberk; and plate armour, which has its origins in the ancient world and was originally comprised of bronze breast plates before evolving into the articulated full-body suits of armour that we normally associate with chivalrous knights in the middle ages. Lamellar armour, another ancient form of military armour, evolved from the earliest use of hardened leathers and hides: a protective material, such as overlaid leather or metal scales, was sewn onto a base material of canvas or leather. Sometimes two or more armours were combined and worn over a close-fitting, sleeveless padded undercoat.

The need to maintain discipline in the ranks by differentiating between them provided a more human imperative for defining military dress. This transcended functionality and enabled military styles to take on a more 'dashing' appearance and visible aesthetic, in turn influencing a wide range of menswear styles through the ages.

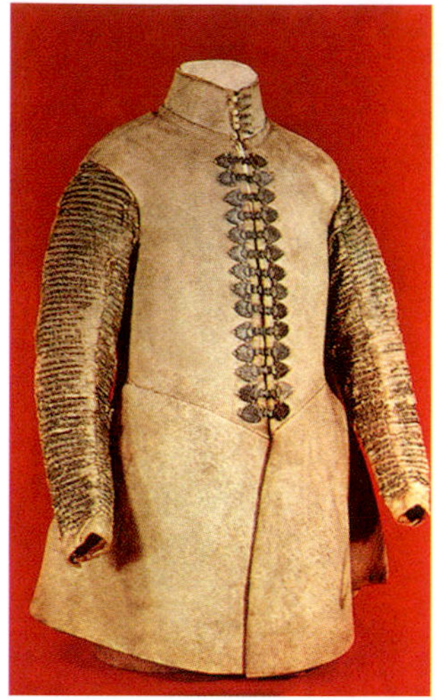

◐ Buff leather jerkin with silver braid on the sleeves as worn by English foot soldiers during the 1620s.

◐ Military wear reinvented and interpreted in street fashion.

◐ French soldiers of the middle ages, taken from A. Racinet's *Historical Costumes*, 1888.

Reefer coat

Reefer coats were originally developed as a form of nautical attire, designed to combat harsh weather conditions. Naval officers wore longer coats, around lower thigh-length, while the sailors' coats were slightly shorter to afford them greater manoeuvrability. The double-breasted reefer coats were styled with traditional anchor buttons and made from heavy melton fabric in dark navy blue and black. The classic reefer style has become a perennial menswear classic as well as a popular fashion item. Authentic naval reefer coats can often be found in army surplus stores and have become assimilated into broader expressions of menswear style.

Duffel coat

The duffel coat is a distinctive, single-breasted hooded coat characterized by horn or wooden toggles, which was originally made from a coarse woollen fabric called duffle. Between the First and Second World Wars, the duffel coat style was adopted by the Royal Navy, who modified it to the needs of its servicemen. The thick woollen fabric offered warmth and protection from the elements while the toggles could be unfastened even when wearing thick gloves. This three-quarter length coat has two large patch pockets and an extra layer of fabric over the shoulders to prevent water soaking through. Despite its humble origins and military associations, the duffel coat has become a classic wardrobe item for men.

Origins of tailoring

The early technological developments of menswear, through successive processes of trial and creation, have largely evolved from military dress. One of the most significant developments of the middle ages was the advancement of padding and more sophisticated quilting processes, which were applied to a shaped canvas fabric or leather to create a padded jacket called a gambeson. The wearing of armour, and the need to protect the upper body from bruising and chafing, also led to the development of a close-fitting sleeveless bodice garment called a gipon, which was laced at the sides and shaped. The emphasis on protecting the torso meant that the sleeves were attached separately by means of lacings called points.

These evolving jacket styles became more prominent and visible as they developed into the shorter fitting doublet styles of the 16th century for military and civilian dress and the longer buff coats for soldiers, which were made out of rough suede. In this way military styles began to exert a strong influence over civilian modes of male dress as well as enabling the development of more sophisticated shapes and construction techniques.

The synergy between military and civilian styles became particularly evident during the Baroque period of the 17th century and male dress styles owed much to military influences. Cassocks and jerkins were worn with breeches and fashionable deerskin boots with heels and spurs, all set off with an abundance of lace trims at the hems and cuffs. During the mid-17th century the English Civil War saw a new type of professional soldier who would be mobilized to fight where the need was greatest. This marked the beginning of a more organized approach to military dress and custom that most of us would begin to recognize today.

The 18th century heralded a new era of trade and military rivalry between the main European powers. Military dress was defined by codified classifications and prominent military braids, since the cut and shape of the clothing itself remained comparable to men's civilian attire. The basis of the military uniform was the regimental coat, which identified each soldier and his unit, and was adorned with regimental buttons, contrast facings, sleeve cuffs and military braids, which became increasingly elaborate and decorative through to the early 19th century.

Double-breasted blazer

It was standard practice for officers and sailors in the 18th century to wear blue jackets with gold buttons for shore attire. The term blazer became attached to the British frigate *HMS Blazer* when the captain supposedly arranged for his crew to wear the distinctive tailored style in preparation for a visit to the ship by Queen Victoria. Today the navy blazer is a classic item of clothing for men. Available in additional colours for civilian attire, the double-breasted tailored blazer, with its characteristic peak lapels, is popular in wool flannels, worsteds and serge. Military-inspired brass buttons adorn this iconic item, which occupies a unique position in a man's wardrobe somewhere between formal and sportswear.

British Warm

Originally conceived as a military overcoat, this British style was worn by officers during the First World War. The double-breasted overcoat is distinctively tailored in appearance with darts and seam shaping and is characterized by the addition of epaulettes and leather buttons. Lapels are peaked with jetted pockets and an outbreast welt. The knee-length British Warm is usually made from melton wool or a heavy cavalry twill with a centre back vent.

Burberry

Founded by a young draper called Thomas Burberry in 1856, the British luxury brand is most closely associated with its distinctive house check and trenchcoat styles for men and women. Thomas Burberry is credited with inventing and promoting gabardine fabric as a breathable, weatherproof fabric during the 19th century. Burberry soon gained a reputation for outfitting expeditions to extreme weather environments including the Antarctic and Mount Everest. A commission by the British War Office in 1914 led to the development of the classic trenchcoat style for men complete with epaulettes, storm flap and 'D' ring attachments.

Burberry continues to update its signature trenchcoats in its contemporary menswear collections.

Ceremonial dress

By the 18th and 19th centuries firearms were prevalent in warfare and the protective function of uniforms became less important. Decorative military dress and ornate uniforms were established as required formal attire for ceremonial occasions, such as military parades and passing-out ceremonies. Historic items of military clothing and accessories, such as a baldric and sword, plumed hats and sash ribbons, were adopted for ceremonial and state occasions. Even today, military dress that may be described as historical in character is worn to convey authority, stability and tradition.

Similarly, the wearing of robes for legal, municipal and academic office has become an important feature in the evolution of menswear by denoting lineage, continuity and succession. In the UK, for example, High Court judges still wear a style of ceremonial dress that includes a full-length scarlet mantle, trimmed with white fur facings, worn over black court breeches and stockings teamed with black patent leather shoes and steel buckles.

The emblematic uniform of a piper in traditional Scottish dress is a particularly distinctive mode of ceremonial dress. Characterized by a tall feather bonnet, military-style doublet or tunic with braids and a clan brooch, a tartan or plaid kilt worn with a horsehair sporran, hose tops, spats or argyle socks and ghillie brogues, this dignified ceremonial uniform has enjoyed royal favour through the centuries.

Military uniforms in all their forms continue to exert a recurring influence on fashion for men and women as well as being adopted and customized in the name of street style.

19th-century portrait of Porfirio Díaz, Mexican president, in his military uniform.

The 'rules' and conventions of menswear have had the effect, over time, of stabilizing men's clothing styles and repelling some of the vagaries of fashion that we might commonly associate with womenswear. In turn, this has enabled the creation of menswear 'classics' such as the military trench coat, which was made from durable gabardine fabric and was specifically designed for soldiers during the First World War. The trench coat has become an iconic garment and a contemporary fashion classic that has been adapted for both menswear and womenswear.

Contemporary womenswear collections often reference men's styling or classic wardrobe pieces as well as incorporating functional detailing taken from menswear clothing. This can take the form of appropriating a man's style, such as a tuxedo jacket, and interpreting the design for women; it can also be through the use of fabrics such as a pinstripe or traditional tweed, or applying a menswear detail, such as safari-style bellows pockets.

◑ **Katharine Hepburn's independent spirit and personal style borrowed heavily from menswear, including her love of wearing tailored trousers.**

Masculine-inspired dressing has become a recurring feature across many womenswear collections, including the Chloe collection for A/W10.

Androgynous associations

Despite previous attempts by some designers to create unisex clothing during the 1960s and 70s, historically, men's and women's dress styles have differentiated themselves through a continuous re-evaluation of line, proportion and silhouette. Fashion's role in reinforcing gender roles and social stereotypes is well-documented through the centuries. However, in the 20th century designers such as Coco Chanel looked to menswear to advance the cause of womenswear; not only by appropriating jersey as an outerwear fabric for women for the first time but also by creating a distinctly androgynous silhouette with her *garçonne* or boyish look, which shocked polite society.

Androgyny is a recurring theme in fashion's complex visual history and it continues to motivate and inspire fashion designers today. Cultural sources such as popular music, sport and street-styles have also contributed to this anomalous area of fashion. In 2002 the Victoria & Albert museum in London hosted an exhibition entitled Men in Skirts, which traced some of the historical precedents for men wearing draped garments whilst exploring the parameters and conventions of contemporary male dress by considering attempts to reinvent 'skirts for men'.

Icon: David Bowie

David Bowie is a multi-talented musician, actor and producer, whose career and musical influence has endured through the years. His slim frame and chameleon-like ability made Bowie a style setter; he skilfully appropriated an amalgam of looks over the years from the mods to 1970s glam rock and later his soul and techno styles. He influenced the early development of the New Romantic style in the UK during the 1980s; however, it is Bowie's androgynous stage persona as Ziggy Stardust during the 1970s that is often cited as one of his most defining looks during his musical career. Bowie has retained his youthful looks and continues to project a convincing personal style.

Film, music and media have all exerted a significant influence on the evolution and development of menswear, particularly throughout the 20th century, which witnessed the rise of consumerism and popular culture. The 20th century also saw a gradual relaxation of some of the old 'rules' of dress that had defined and contained menswear through the previous centuries. The impetus for change often came through sporting and leisure activities as well as through musical traditions, which were being communicated to wider audiences. After the traumatic years of the First World War, Europe and America were ready to embrace change. The growth and popularity of American Hollywood films was particularly significant in the evolution of menswear and enabled a more relaxed mode of dress to gain wider acceptance. The American lounge suit grew in popularity as the class-based frock-coat was consigned to formal occasions and the margins of fashionable dress.

Icon: James Dean

James Dean is the undisputed 'rebel without a cause' after starring in the acclaimed movie of the same name. His untimely death came in a car crash in 1955 at the tender age of 24. In dying so young, Dean's legacy was assured and it is inextricably linked to the angst of disaffected youth and the emergence of the post-war teenager. Dean helped to popularize denim jeans and defined the teenage look for a generation.

Film

Just as it had done for women, Hollywood helped to define and redefine male dress styles, thanks to the popularity of screen icons such as Clark Gable, Fred Astaire, Gary Cooper and Cary Grant. Hollywood was also responsible for introducing American cowboy and mob gangster styles to European audiences. The new teenage rebel was soon to follow in the form of screen icons James Dean and Marlon Brando, both of whom also popularized Levis 501 denim jeans by wearing them on-screen. Film media continued to project images of menswear and dress styles that not only reflected the mood of the period but also set trends that influenced retailers, designers and consumers. In the early 1980s Italian designer Giorgio Armani influenced a generation of men with his sleek Italian suits and established himself in the United States when he designed Richard Gere's on-screen wardrobe in the film *American Gigolo*. The 1980s television show *Miami Vice* captured the zeitgeist of the period with its deconstructed jackets and pastel tones for men. Today, actors such as Brad Pitt and Johnny Depp continue to influence menswear with their on-screen and personal style.

Icon: Brad Pitt

After gaining wider public recognition for his supporting role as a svelte cowboy drifter in Ridley Scott's 1991 road movie *Thelma & Louise*, Brad Pitt quickly emerged as a media-promoted sex symbol and the man other men aspired to imitate with his cool persona, easy charm and good looks. Subsequent movies have established Pitt as a modern male icon with a transferable style that fits the mood and the occasion. His ability to adapt his appearance and dress style from casual and sporty to more formal and red carpet occasions, have assured his place in contemporary menswear iconography.

Media

The 1980s also saw a resurgence of interest in men's fashion through fashion and lifestyle magazines including *GQ*, *i-D*, *The Face*, *Uomo Vogue* and *Esquire*. These publications brought a wider view of fashion to men and women by expanding the view of menswear beyond what was locally available in the stores to more aspirational, global and multi-lifestyle directions. The magazines also served to challenge, as well as reinforce, male stereotypes by addressing issues of class, race, sexual orientation and body type through editorial and corporate advertising. Billboard advertising took on a special significance with designers using high-profile stars in their campaigns, such as a recent advert for Giorgio Armani, which featured sports star and style icon David Beckham.

More recently the Internet and ever more sophisticated digital mobile communications have extended the range and impact of conventional menswear media channels. This has been particularly evident in the growth of blogs featuring 'real people' photographed in the street. Blogs such as Stylesightings and The Sartorialist continue to redefine the relationship between menswear and the fashion media in the 21st century.

Music

Music holds a special place in the evolution and development of modern menswear. It has a special ability to converge with fashion, spanning style and musical genres, product endorsement and style icons from The Beatles and David Bowie to Snoop Dog and Kanye West. Since the launch of MTV in 1981, music has also embraced mass media culture and reinforced established and new peer group allegiances and musical cultures from heavy metal to hip hop and more. See pages 40–49 for music's influences on counter-culture dressing.

The Beatles during their critically acclaimed Sgt Pepper incarnation, wearing colourful psychedelic military-inspired uniforms.

A counter culture is one that reacts against the mainstream culture of the time, causing societal change. A counter culture is different in its politics, norms, social beliefs, social structures and, importantly in this context, its way of dress. Here we examine various counter cultures and their influence on menswear and fashion.

Zoot suits

One of the earliest examples of a fashion-orientated subculture for men was the wearing of zoot suits during the late 1930s and 1940s. The style was popularized by young African Americans and Latino Americans during this period and had originated among the dance halls where some of the more athletic dancers took up the jitterbug dance. The suit became a symbol of self determination among some minority groups and was an extreme form of the looser-fitting lounge jacket with wide shoulder padding, wide lapels and additional length through the body of the jacket. Worn in combination with a high-waisted pair of trousers, which were pegged at the hem to be very narrow at the ankles, the overall proportions were pronounced and exaggerated. The zoot suit was in fact sometimes a sports jacket and trousers with an open-neck shirt splayed over the top collar of the jacket. For special occasions it would be a suit, often in flamboyant colours and stripes, worn in combination with a waistcoat, shirt and tie with optional watch chain.

This film still from *Stormy Weather* shows American jazz singer and big band leader Cab Calloway in a zoot suit, worn with a bow tie and watch chain.

The teddy boy look endured; this image, taken in 1972, shows a group of Teds dancing at the London rock and roll revival show in Wembley Arena.
Michael Webb / Hutton Archive / Getty Images

The defined teddy boy look has been revived by designers and musicians alike, as shown in this A/W10 collection by Bottega Veneta.

Teddy boys

Originating in post-war London in the late 1940s and early 1950s, the British teddy boy or 'Ted' emerged as a working-class fashion for younger men, inspired by the sartorial style of the Edwardian dandies from the 1900s. Teddy boys wore longer-fitting draped jackets, cuffed sleeves, waistcoats and narrow 'drainpipe' trousers. Their favoured footwear was either brogues or crepe-soled shoes. Teddy boys became the first definable youth subculture in the UK, appealing to those young men who didn't want to dress like their fathers. Musically they associated themselves with American rock and roll and soon gained notoriety in the press with their alleged antisocial behaviour in movie theatres and dance halls. From a style perspective the look endured, with a core following that remained loyal to it.

Mods and rockers

Because of their gang rivalries and opposing dress styles during the 1960s, mods and rockers emerged in the UK as two distinct counter-cultures. The mods (the term is derived from modernist) favoured trim-fitting Italian suits and projected a clean, well-turned out dandy style. Jacket lapels were typically narrow; suit materials included mohair and two-tone fabrics, worn in combination with button-down shirts, sweaters, slim trousers and pointed shoes known as winklepickers. Mods listened to American soul music and Jamaican ska and developed their own British musical style. They popularized the use of the red, white and blue target symbol as badges or logos on their parka jackets and Vespa scooters. The mods' rivals were the unkempt-looking rockers, who wore black leather biker jackets and jeans and rode heavy motorcycles. As their name suggests, the rockers aligned themselves to American rock and roll music. They had much less regard for their general appearance or grooming. Rivalry between these opposing British counter cultures was a preoccupation of newspapers for a short period during the 1960s until public interest and media attention faded.

In the UK, rockers were often engaged in brawls with mods. In May 1964 mods and rockers were jailed after riots in seaside resorts on the south coast of England.

Skinheads

Skinheads originated as a youth counter culture in the UK during the mid-1960s. Their appearance was characterized by their close-cropped or shaved heads and their pronounced allegiance to a dress code that included specific brands such as Ben Sherman, Brutus or polo shirts worn with braces and Sta-Prest trousers or straight-fitting denim jeans with turn-ups. The look was sometimes finished off with a Crombie-style top coat and Dr. Martens lace-up boots or loafers. Their appearance was uncompromisingly tough in contrast to the vagaries of the hippie culture. Skinheads originally evolved from British mods (see page 43). Today skinheads have evolved into disparate groups across the world with their own interpretation of this counter culture.

Harrington jacket

British clothing company Baracuta originated the Harrington jacket, known as the G9, in the 1930s. The iconic style has an impressive pedigree of celebrity wearers that include Steve McQueen, James Dean, Elvis Presley and more recently Pete Doherty and Damon Albarn. The name 'Harrington' was later derived from the surname of Ryan O'Neal's character in the 1960s American drama *Peyton Place*. The short-fitting blouson jacket is characterized by a Fraser tartan lining, centre-front zipper opening with raglan sleeves and snug wrap-over button stand collar. Adopted during the 1960s by mods and skinheads, the Harrington jacket has a unique street credibility that continues to endure and inspire new generations.

Skinheads and hippies in London's Piccadilly in the late 1960s. The skinhead appearance was uncompromisingly tough in contrast to the vagaries of hippie culture.

Hippies

The term hippie, originally derived from the word 'hipster', was soon applied to a member of the youth movement that emerged in the United States during the mid-1960s. A hippie was a man or woman whose values were broadly liberal and who favoured commune lifestyles, mysticism and the use of drugs to enhance consciousness. As a movement it spread to Europe and beyond and attracted men and women of all ages.

Hippies dressed in a bohemian style that accommodated individual discretion, but which broadly adopted the wearing of denim jeans, customized clothing, long hair for men, sandals, fringed clothing with craft-adornment and multicoloured effects that rejected the conventions of fashion. Although the term 'hippie' became somewhat derisory over time, its enduring legacy is more musical than stylistic since its ethos was to reject mainstream fashion.

Glam rock

Glam rock describes a style that emerged in the UK during the 1970s; its playful nod to androgyny was popularized by artists and musicians such as David Bowie and Marc Bolan. The look was deliberately excessive and colourful and included the wearing of platform shoes or boots as well as all-in-one jump suits for men and women. Glam rock style was characterized by flamboyance and theatricality, which was largely driven by the excesses of the pop stars of the period who pushed the boundaries with their stage acts and appearances on television. Although the glam rock style didn't endure into the 1980s, during its brief run it liberated menswear by allowing the usual 'rules' of dressing to be relaxed or broken. Destined to burn itself out, glam rock was ultimately usurped by the arrival of punk rock.

Punk rock

Punk rockers, also known as 'punks', emerged in the UK and USA during the 1970s and immediately attracted attention and notoriety with their extreme appearance, which included outlandish spiked hairstyles in dyed colours, body piercings, torn or slashed clothes, graphic T-shirt prints and bondage trousers. Clashing combinations of neon colours, animal prints and leathers also characterized the punk style. Closely associated with punk rock music, the counter culture embraced both sexes and even flirted with cross-gender looks; however, the predominantly tough appearance of the punks lent itself to a rebellious menswear style that rejected the conventions of fashion. Designer Vivienne Westwood and Malcolm McLaren, manager of the Sex Pistols, famously helped to define the UK punk style with their early collections, which were sold in their shop on the Kings Road in London. Subsequent designers have drawn inspiration from the punk movement including Jean Paul Gaultier, who appropriated the tartan kilt as a fashionable item of menswear.

Marc Bolan, lead singer of T. Rex in the 1970s, helped shape the glam rock era.

Punks sought to outrage others with their tough, anarchic style.
Dave Hogan / Hutton Archive / Getty Images

Leather biker jacket

The black leather biker jacket is a menswear classic with an all-American heritage. Although many styles and variations exist today, the introduction of the original double breasted, black leather, zipper-front jacket by Schott Bros in 1928 heralded an instant classic. The Schott company called their new jacket the Perfecto. Originally made from horse hide, the jacket was soon manufactured in steer hide and adorned with a belt buckle, cuff zippers and snaps (press stud fastenings) for durability and style. From the outset the leather biker jacket represented and inspired a sense of freedom and adventure, before gaining its iconic status in 1953, when Marlon Brando wore a Perfecto leather jacket in the movie *The Wild One*. The rebellious associations continued when it was worn by rockers in the 1960s and punks in the 1980s. Admired and imitated over the years, the Perfecto biker jacket is a true classic.

New Romantics

This music-inspired subculture emerged in the UK in the late 1970s, mainly among disaffected art school graduates who shared a love for David Bowie and Roxy Music's flamboyant and sometimes gender-ambiguous stage style and music. Soon the subculture developed its own musical style from a strong nightclub tradition. The look was characterized by androgynous clothing, sashes and ruffles, with the men wearing conspicuous make-up and arranging their hair upwards into quiffs or pouf styles, which heralded in the big hair looks of the 1980s. Musically, the nightclub scene developed its own style and acts but ultimately fell victim to its own sense of exclusiveness, which limited its lasting appeal. Today, the New Romantics are strongly associated with the early 1980s and an age of excess and foppish menswear.

▲ The New Romantic scene emerged largely from nightclub Billy's, in London, which ran David Bowie and Roxy Music nights in the late 1970s.

Hip hop trio Run-DMC personified the early hip hop style of the 1980s with their tracksuits, bucket hats, gold jewellery and trainers.

Hip hop

Hip hop first emerged during the 1970s in the United States among African American and Latino American youth communities. It has gone on to define itself in successive decades through its assimilation of street styles and an evolving music culture, which commands loyalty and devotion from its followers. With its original links to street art, graffiti and urban music, early hip hop style was characterized by oversized bomber jackets, baggy jeans and graffiti-inspired prints on T-shirts and sweat tops.

Men's hip hop style began to accommodate alternative expressions of style during the early 2000s. This included more designer labels, such as Gucci and Louis Vuitton, combined with personalized, often ostentatious jewellery. Style is an integral component of the hip hop culture, which has seen the evolution of its own design labels including Phat Farm, Sean John and Rocawear. Unlike other subcultures, hip hop continues to redefine itself without compromising its meaning or values.

Heritage Research

Who are the names behind Heritage Research?

Heritage Research is owned and designed by myself (Russ Gater) and Daniel Savory. We create the concept each season, research and re-work the garments and source the fabric and trims. The patterns are made and cut by an ex-Savile Row tailor who trained in the 1950s, the golden age of tailoring! The garments are then assembled by a small team of seasoned crafts people.

What does the label stand for?

We originally started HR in 2008 almost as a reaction to the over-branding and homogenized look of many labels. It began as a side project with the view to create a small brand that was entirely about the form and fit of the garment, offering an almost bespoke made-to-order piece through selected stores. We wanted to create garments that properly referenced original historical pieces, not just in an aesthetic way but also in cut, fabric and construction; however, we also acknowledged they would have to fit into a contemporary wardrobe and be worn alongside more modern styles. We decided early on that HR would have no branding or logo and so would be purely about the garment.

Where do you get your inspiration from?

A lot of the ideas are based on pieces in our own collections. Some of the older referenced garments such as the naval artillery jacket (based on a federal sack jacket from the American Civil War) are more difficult to actually source and come from books, old photos or museums. We tend not to have a single theme for any collection, which allows us to bring a variety of eras and styles into each selection.

I'm always surprised by the sheer functionality of a lot of historical garments. They were born out of a time of necessity, designed for a specific purpose – to function and protect under adverse and challenging conditions using what was available. Especially interesting is clothing that was adapted at home, such as a hunting jacket or work shirt, altered to enable that person to do their job better. Obviously during World War 2 boundaries were pushed to create new fabrics, such as Ventile, and garments were made under contract for every required function, some of them so good they remain in use today.

Please outline your current job and career path.

I am the creative director of Lou Dalton Menswear. After leaving school at the age of 16 I enrolled as an apprentice to a bespoke tailor. After three successful years I realized that to fulfil my long-term ambition of becoming a menswear designer I would need to enrol back into education. I studied fashion design and then applied to the Royal College of Art to study a Master of Arts in Menswear design. Upon graduating from the RCA in 1998 I moved out to Italy to work for a design studio based in Bologna called Alexandro Pungetti, which created collections for various Italian design companies; I personally worked on collections for Stone Island, Crucianni Knitwear and Iceberg.

After a year I returned to London and worked for various design companies. Back in 2005 I started to play around with the idea of creating my own menswear collection. Lou Dalton came into fruition in late 2008 and since then seems to be going from strength to strength, with wonderful support from the press, the British Fashion Council and, most importantly, the retailers.

Where do you get your inspiration from?

Anywhere and everywhere, like most designers; it could be from a book, an exhibition, being on vacation, a vintage find. The A/W10 collection was inspired by a family holiday to the wonderful Isle of Skye. I was totally taken away with this place; it was so inspiring. The most recent S/S11 collection was inspired by the nomadic lifestyle along with the turbulent life of Heathcliff from *Wuthering Heights*, who started out as a street urchin...

How do you update your collections?

With menswear it's not necessarily about redesigning the wheel every season; you get a feeling for what your customer is looking for. I try to have some link between each season, even if it is a little vague at times. My main consideration is always, is it relevant? There has to be a sense of commerciality, the importance of each piece from the collection being able to stand alone as well as within the collection. A new selection of fabrics and yarns each season helps instantly to update a collection, without necessarily redesigning a great pair of trousers from the season before, that sold remarkably well. It is important to offer something new to help engage support from your customer base.

If people turn to look at you on the street, you are not well dressed.

Beau Brummell

2

Having considered the broad historical traditions and influences that have shaped menswear through the ages, this chapter addresses the distinctive nature and character of men's tailoring. The more formal protocols of male dressing, including the modern evolution of men's trousers, shirts, neck dressings and shoes, are examined in detail. It is interesting to compare and contrast the nature of bespoke tailoring in the context of national characteristics and international centres of excellence; there is a section on notable tailoring houses and sartorial firms in the UK, Italy and the United States for further research.

The origins of the modern men's suit can be traced back to the mid-17th century with the introduction of the cassock (casaque) coat for men. The new, longer fitting style was worn with a matching waistcoat (known as a vest in the US) and it was enthusiastically adopted by King Charles II in England. The eminent diarist Samuel Pepys wrote on 8 October 1666, 'The king hath yesterday in Council declared his resolution of setting a fashion for clothes, which he will never alter...'.

Pepys went on to refer to Eastern modes of dress derived from Persia, which historians believe to be the basis of the cassock style, probably introduced to European courts by ambassadors to Persia and the Middle East. By publicly announcing his break from established men's clothing styles King Charles was also asserting his independence from the dominant French court styles set by King Louis XIV. However, the French king had also adopted the new casaque style almost simultaneously and within a few years the new coat had gained widespread acceptance.

Portrait of Captain Wade, 1771, wearing a fashionable cutaway coat with long decorative waistcoat and close-fitting knee breeches.

Example of a three-piece sack suit as worn by an Englishman, 1904, teamed with a bowler hat and stiffened detachable shirt collar and neck tie.

The cassock

The cassock signalled the demise of the doublet jacket and, more significantly, established a new proportion for men, cut in one piece from the shoulder to the hem and worn in combination with a long waistcoat and breeches. Lace cravats and tied neck dressings took on a new importance. What followed were a series of variations of this three-piece combination with English and French styles competing for style supremacy, just as the two countries competed for political and territorial influence.

Adaptations of the cassock style evolved into a variety of jackets. Horsehair canvases were used as interlinings to add support to the evolving tailored silhouettes. Cutaway fronts on jackets were refined and early examples of the stand-fall collar were introduced, so-named because the collar was turned down over its stand. Waistcoats became shorter and close-fitting knee breeches were fashionably worn with riding boots. The English perfected the riding habit, which would later be adapted by Beau Brummell in the early 19th century (see page 64).

By the early 19th century the accepted combination of a jacket, waistcoat and trousers formed the basis of a man's mode of dress. Fabrics varied according to the occasion or time of day, but when the jacket and trouser were cut from the same fabric it was referred to as a 'suit', as it is today.

▲ ▼ A bespoke suit made on Savile Row will take a minimum of 50 hours of handwork and involves a series of fittings.

Bespoke

Bespoke is an English word derived from the past tense of bespeak, meaning to reserve or order something in advance; it is now used to describe clothing that is custom made. Bespoke clothing, made to a client's individual specifications, is associated with a high level of craftsmanship and service.

The Savile Row Bespoke Association's definition of bespoke is a suit made on or around Savile Row, bespoken to the customer's specifications. A bespoke suit is cut by an individual and made by highly skilled craftsmen, using a pattern that is drafted specifically for the customer. In the finest traditions of menswear, Savile Row bespoke can be compared to French haute couture: custom-made womenswear in accordance with the definitions of the Fédération Française De La Couture. See page 68 for more on Savile Row.

Tweed jacket

Often associated with a British-inspired country style, tweed jackets are usually single breasted with a two- or three-button front opening, flap pockets and a centre-back vent reminiscent of a riding jacket, and occasionally leather buttons and elbow patches. Some American and continental Europeans favour side-back vents and a slightly more relaxed construction. A tweed jacket represents a link with tradition and continuity, while accommodating different individual styles, occasions and tastes through an extensive range of cloth designs including Harris tweed, Donegal tweed, herringbone tweed, houndstooth pattern and shepherd's check.

Single-breasted blazer

The single-breasted blazer evolved from the English rowing clubs of the 19th century. The most popular versions are navy blue with brass or enamel buttons, but they are also available in a variety of club stripes and bright colours, in cotton twills and linens; sometimes edged with braid and styled with patch pockets. The style has been adopted in the US as a preppy look and also picked up by menswear designers who may add a badge to the out-breast pocket. A classic combination of navy blazer and grey flannel trousers is a mark of sporting sobriety.

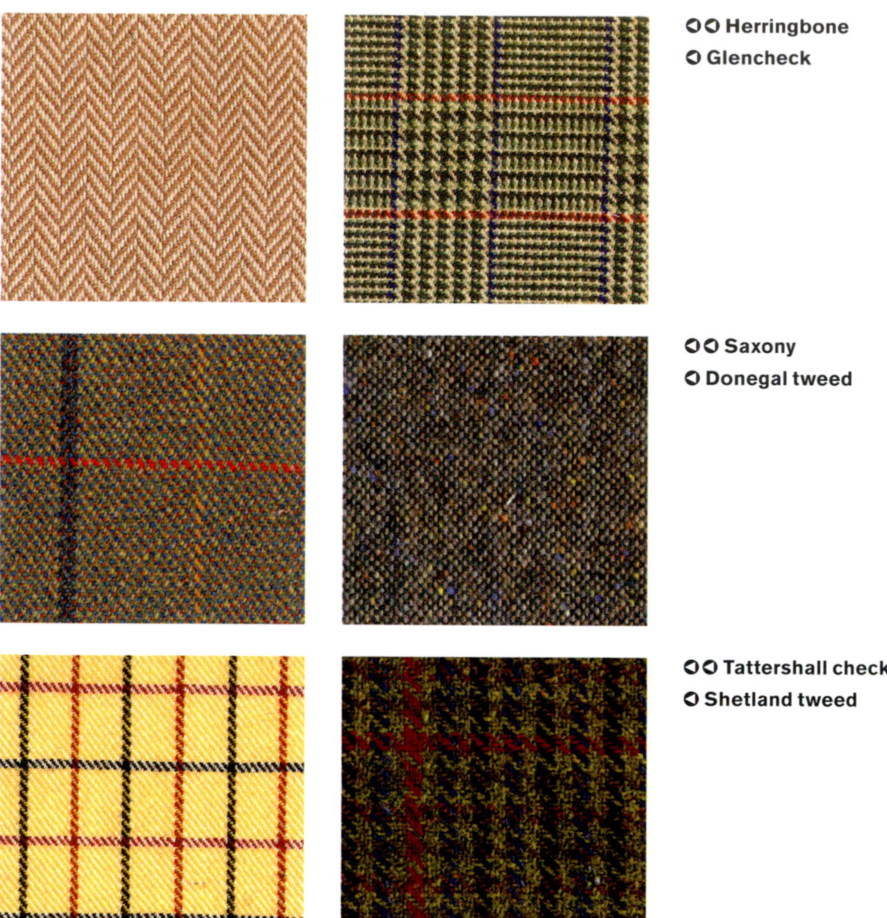

◀◀ Herringbone
◀ Glencheck

◀◀ Saxony
◀ Donegal tweed

◀◀ Tattershall check
◀ Shetland tweed

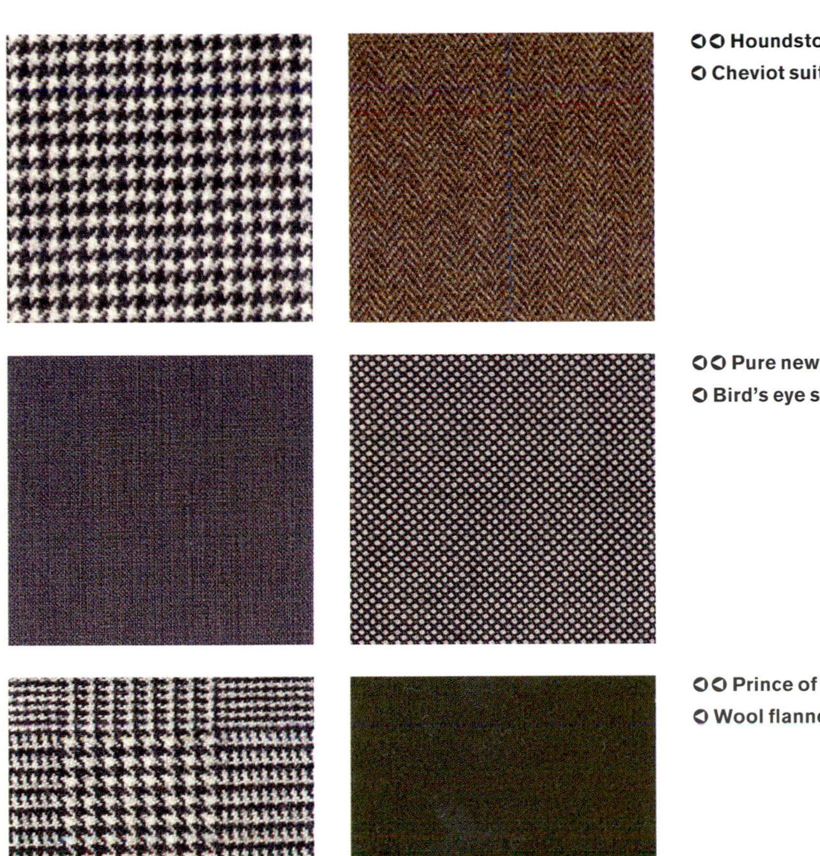

◐◐ Houndstooth check
◐ Cheviot suiting

◐◐ Pure new wool suiting
◐ Bird's eye suiting

◐◐ Prince of Wales check
◐ Wool flannel

The history of menswear includes references to some notable individuals and male groups that have distinguished themselves in matters of dressing and their associated behaviour. Foremost among such classifications are the macaronis and the dandies.

Dandy

As a lay definition, a dandy is usually applied to the description of a man who takes great care and pride in his appearance and who is also capable of articulate discussion and witty repartee. Although 'dandies' were reputedly in existence since the Restoration period in England (mid-17th century) the word 'dandy' entered the collective English vocabulary during the 18th century. Among the most notable dandies of their ages are George 'Beau' Brummell, Oscar Wilde and Robert de Montesquiou. Closely associated with the wearing of fine tailored clothing, contemporary dandies proudly continue a long-standing tradition of sartorial individuality.

Sapeurs

Sapeurs are a contemporary phenomenon in the best traditions of the dandy. The name 'Sapeur' is derived from SAPE, an acronym for Société des Ambianceurs et Persons Elégants. Originating in the central African Republic of Congo, specifically in parts of the Congolese capital Brazzaville, Sapeurs can be traced back to the 1920s and 30s when Congo was a French colony. During this time an elite number of Congolese men visited Paris to experience the fashion elegance of the French capital and returned to Congo with their selection of highly prized suits and jackets. Favouring striking colours and dapper cuts, but always with a reverence for the most exclusive French and European designer labels, the so called 'cult of the cloth' was established as part of the Sapeur creed. As well as emphasizing individual style, Sapeurs are respected members of their local communities and consider themselves to be artists.

○ In the true spirit of dandyism, Sapeur outfits are carefully chosen and immaculately worn on a daily basis, with fastidious attention to detail.

Icon: Beau Brummell

George Bryan Brummell, better known as Beau Brummell, is one of the most noted and celebrated figures in the evolution of menswear, particularly sartorial clothing.

Following the turbulences of the French Revolution, English clothing styles for men grew in popularity and influence during the early decades of the 19th century. At the same time in England, Beau Brummell was also in his ascendancy as a fashion arbiter of good taste and refinement. Brummell moved in influential circles and gained favour with the Prince Regent and future King George IV of England. Before his association with Brummell the Prince Regent was known for his ostentatious style; however, Brummell is widely credited with moderating the future King's ornate dress sense. The Prince Regent's approval meant that English aristocrats soon adopted more sober styles of dressing; bright colours, decorative emblems and high heels all soon went out of fashion for gentlemen.

Brummell's greatest talent was that he reworked existing styles and combinations rather than introducing completely new garments. He adapted English country styles, such as the men's riding habit, and made them appear new and relevant for city dressing by changing them from red to navy or black and by refining proportions. He also popularized the wearing of long trousers rather than knee breeches and paid great attention to neckwear dressings.

Brummell left an enduring legacy in the story and future direction of menswear. Today he is remembered with his own statue in Jermyn Street in London, a smart area notable for its concentration of fine menswear establishments.

Macaroni

Derived from an Italian word to describe a boorish fool, the word macaroni was adopted in England during the mid-18th century as a derisory term to describe a man of fashion who dressed and behaved in an affected manner that was characterized by levels of pomposity and flamboyance beyond accepted norms. Striking in their outward appearance and providing rich content for caricatures of the period, macaronis have been unfairly cited as the heirs apparent to dandies although the two groups and definitions are quite different from each other.

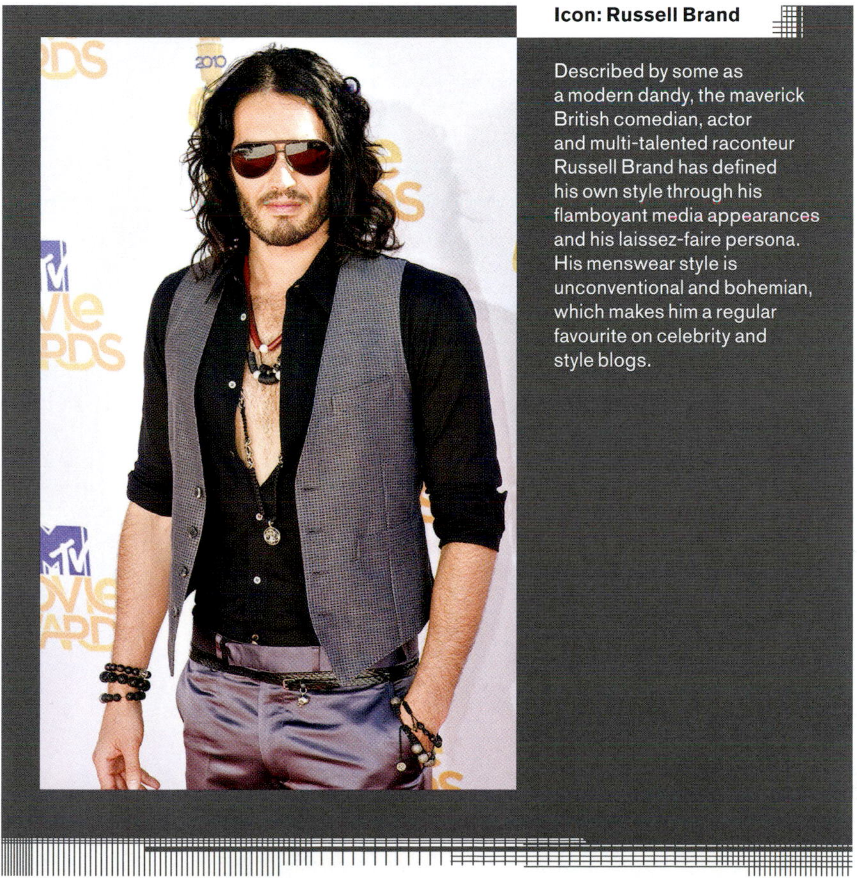

Icon: Russell Brand

Described by some as a modern dandy, the maverick British comedian, actor and multi-talented raconteur Russell Brand has defined his own style through his flamboyant media appearances and his laissez-faire persona. His menswear style is unconventional and bohemian, which makes him a regular favourite on celebrity and style blogs.

British tailoring emerged in its own right during the early 19th century as *'le style Anglais'* or the English look. This coincided with the UK's economic ascendancy through expanding trade and the momentum of the Industrial Revolution. The notion of communicating one's social status and rank through the cut, fit, details and style of men's clothing was the accepted practice of the 19th and early 20th century. Consequently, the British suit is associated with an enduring formality expressed through an exacting cut, fit and fabrication, which sets it apart from its Italian or American counterparts.

English suits were traditionally cut with a slightly high waist; high, close-fitting armholes and long vents, allowing the jacket tails to fall gently over the hips. This so-called 'hourglass' cut owed much to the historical development of English riding habits and military uniform jackets. It also enforced the principle of standing up straight and good posture, a valued indicator of a man's character. The formal English cut tended to flatter taller, slim men who were more likely to be considered as gentlemen or officer class. Tailored trousers were cut to rest high on the hips and sit relatively close to the leg. Braces were much favoured over belts and served to elongate the torso, while the flattering high waist created the impression of longer legs.

During the 19th century, many tailors in London organized themselves into firms to meet the burgeoning demand to dress city merchants. So began British tailoring's special association with Savile Row.

Chesterfield

A city topcoat for gentlemen that was originally worn during the 19th century, the Chesterfield has retained a level of formality that makes it suitable for wearing over a suit. It is a single-breasted style with a concealed button front opening, most commonly in a grey, blue or black herringbone pattern and sometimes trimmed with a velvet top collar.

○ Since opening his first store in Nottingham, England, in 1970, Sir Paul Smith has become a pre-eminent British designer, particularly well-known for his menswear collections. His international reputation as a designer is centred on a distinctly English style that is infused with a playful sensibility, which is often associated with multi-stripe trims and colourful detailing but always with a respect for classic English tailoring.

Iconic London street sign for Savile Row, the epicentre of men's bespoke tailoring.

Savile Row

Savile Row is a street in London's Mayfair district that has developed as the geographic hub for the UK's finest tailors. (It is also known as the location for The Beatles' last gig on the rooftop of their London headquarters.) Savile Row is first and foremost a bastion of sartorial British style, representing the highest standards of quality and service; its exceptional tailoring heritage is over 200 years old.

In accordance with the Savile Row Bespoke Association, Savile Row bespoke firms should:

- Individually cut a paper pattern produced by a Master Cutter
- Have personal supervision of production by the Master Cutter
- Have cutters and tailors trained to the exacting standards of Savile Row
- Typically create a two-piece suit almost completely by hand – with at least 50 hours of hand work
- Provide an expert cloth consultant on the premises
- Offer a choice of a least 2,000 fabrics to the customer, which may include a range of exclusive cloths
- Retain full customer records and order details
- Provide first-class aftercare for garments including sponging, pressing, repairs and button matching

Ordering a bespoke suit from Savile Row used to be a very exclusive affair, requiring a formal introduction to one of the tailoring firms by an existing client. Although such formal etiquettes have been relaxed over the years, Savile Row's exacting standards remain intact as an assurance of quality. Suits must include the following features:

- Hand-cut and shaped shoulder pads and canvases
- Top collar draw-stitched by hand on to the facing
- Front edges and vents prick-stitched by hand
- Sleeves set in by hand
- Front and cuff buttons sewn on by hand with cross stitch
- All linings felled by hand
- Armhole lining eased and hand-felled
- Front pockets top-stitched by hand
- Cuffs with open slit and hand-stitched buttonholes
- Slanting breast pocket with hand-stitched border
- Sufficient inlays to allow a 3in adjustment to the main body seams

'The only man who behaved sensibly was my tailor; he took my measurement anew every time he saw me, while all the rest went on with their old measurements and expected them to fit me.'
George Bernard Shaw

A fully bespoke Savile Row suit is handmade to a client's specifications on the tailor's premises, by Savile Row trained craftsmen after a full set of measurements have been taken. This involves a series of fittings over 4–12 weeks. These days most Savile Row tailors also offer a personal tailoring service and a ready-to-wear line with alteration options as well as selling gentlemen's accessories.

Despite the proliferation and availability of menswear designer labels today, Savile Row has not only survived through turbulent economic times but is finding new favour and a new clientele that value the unique proposition that it represents. Some of the more notable names in Savile Row are featured on the following pages.

◐ ◑ ◓ Anderson & Sheppard has been following the traditions of Savile Row tailoring since 1906, through its bespoke service.

Richard Anderson

Richard Anderson and Brian Lishak are the co-founders and names behind this esteemed bespoke tailoring house on Savile Row. Both master tailors had worked on Savile Row for many years before combining their considerable talents and establishing the label in 2001. Working with the finest cloths to traditional Savile Row methods, the Richard Anderson label produces tailoring with an elegant line that is long and flattering to the figure with a high cut armhole.

Anderson & Sheppard

This discreet tailoring house, which is reputed to make suits for Prince Charles, has resisted all offers to license its name and does not present a ready-to-wear collection. Anderson & Sheppard symbolizes what many would consider to be the mystique and allure of Savile Row. The house style is a lightly padded shoulder, draped chest and gently defined waist. All lapels are hand padded and seams kept to a minimum in order to better display the finery of their cloths.

Ozwald Boateng

Ozwald Boateng has acquired a reputation for presenting a modern, colourful expression of Savile Row's sartorial style. With a crisp, structured cut and an attention to detail, Boateng has gained patronage from an impressive list of fashion, media and celebrity clients. Boateng's view of menswear is international, which is in part a reflection of his Ghanaian heritage. He presents his named 'bespoke-couture' collections in Milan, Italy.

Chester Barrie

Selling classic, English hand-tailored suits since 1937, Chester Barrie maintains a workshop on Savile Row and a factory in Crewe, a town in northern England. The firm acquired a reputation for high quality and craftsmanship by combining skilled machine operations with hand-cutting techniques. The special proposition of Chester Barrie was to produce high-quality ready-to-wear clothing using traditional English tailoring methods. In 1981 Savile Row tailors H Huntsman (see page 72) ordered their first ready-to-wear stock from Chester Barrie.

Dege & Skinner

Established in 1865, this well-respected tailoring firm represents the finest traditions of Savile Row with close links to the British Royal family, the Sultan of Oman and King of Bahrain. The house style is characterized by a long-waisted jacket with sloping shoulders, which reflects the firm's military cutting expertise: it has contracts to make British Royal Horse Artillery dress jackets, pantaloons and ceremonial tunics for officers of the Household Cavalry and the Brigade of Guards.

Ede & Ravenscroft

Founded in 1689, Ede and Ravenscroft is the oldest tailor in London and thought to be the oldest firm of tailors in the world. With long-established links to British royalty, the company also provides tailoring and robe making services to the church, state and legal profession, as well as for academia.

Gieves & Hawkes

With its flagship store occupying the prestigious 1 Savile Row premises, Gieves & Hawkes has been operating since 1786. Early clients included Admiral Lord Nelson and the Duke of Wellington. Today the firm continues to offer its top-of-the-range bespoke tailoring service as well as a flexible ready-to-wear service with a range of additional service options. The firm's custom tailors are trained in providing a high-quality measuring and fitting service that caters to individual client specifications.

H Huntsman & Sons

Established in 1849, H Huntsman & Sons specialize in gentlemen's hunting wear and riding habits; they are known for their close-fitting jackets and defined waists. All of Huntsman's bespoke tailored clothing is hand-crafted on the premises and is renowned for its meticulous attention to detail.

Richard James

Since opening their Savile Row premises in 1992, Richard James and business partner Sean Dixon have adopted a thoroughly modern approach to their business by offering contemporary made-to-measure suits and gentlemen's accessories in addition to the firm's bespoke service. The tailoring label's signature long-waisted, slim silhouette and contemporary use of colour have attracted many admirers and enabled the business to appeal to new generations of menswear customers. This has included opening a stand-alone store in Tokyo and the addition of Richard James Bespoke opposite the firm's original Savile Row premises.

Kilgour

Since announcing its presence on Savile Row in 1882, Kilgour developed a steady reputation for its tailoring craftsmanship. The tailoring house acquired links with some of Hollywood's elite including Louis B Meyer and Cary Grant, who was a loyal patron. Kilgour's house style and signature one-button jackets suited Cary Grant's elegant frame. Today the company continues to offer both bespoke and ready-to-wear collections and a full alterations service that draws on the firm's bespoke heritage.

◀ ▼ **Contemporary one-button velvet suit jacket and slender fitting two-button front blue cotton stripe summer jacket, both by Richard James.**

Norton & Sons

Established in 1821 by Walter Norton as tailors to gentlemen of the City of London, the tailoring firm enjoyed rapid growth during the 19th century before moving to Savile Row in the 1860s. The firm soon distinguished itself with its classically cut tailoring and use of lighter weight cloths for overseas travel, along with its extensive range of sartorial styles, including lounge suits, dinner suits, morning coats, shooting jackets and field coats.

Henry Poole

Founded in 1806, the illustrious tailoring house of Henry Poole located to its Savile Row premises in 1846 and gained patronage with clients including Emperor Napoleon III, Charles Dickens and Edward VII. Awarded the royal warrant for making state liveries by Queen Victoria, Henry Poole reopened its livery department to make garments for coachmen and footmen as well as producing ceremonial dress and court dress for High Sheriffs.

Icon: Mick Jagger

Musician, writer and singing legend Mick Jagger has enjoyed a long career with his band the Rolling Stones. As the front man for the band his style has often been reported through the media. Beneath his rebellious exterior and flirtations with androgyny, Jagger has always appreciated sartorial style. He favours the more radical tailors of Savile Row, such as Edward Sexton, the master cutter at Tommy Nutter, who famously made the three-piece suit for his wedding to Bianca Jagger in 1971, and modern tailors, such as Ozwald Boateng and Richard James.

Italy holds a unique position in the evolution and development of European menswear, endorsed by a long-standing tradition of high-quality textile weaving skills and craftsmanship. Italy's unification during the 19th century reveals regional differences that still define Italian suit makers. Even during the Renaissance, the Italian states distinguished themselves from their northern European neighbours by lacking a central court structure. At ease with the notions of personal display and regional individuality, Italian men have gained a culturally informed view of dressing that asserts the right of the individual to dress up over any preoccupations of class.

Italian suit makers are known for their refinement and lightness of touch, which they equate with elegance, revealed through the use of lightweight fabrics and interlinings that fall outside the tradition of Savile Row. Colours are also light and airy in comparison to traditional British textiles, reflecting not only a gentler weather climate but also Italian men's attitudes to wearing a suit as a marker of taste and lifestyle over personal wealth or class. Fellini's 1960 movie *La Dolce Vita* personified this attitude and confirmed Italy's post-war revival as a centre for fine men's tailoring.

Today, Italy's world-renowned suit makers can be loosely divided between its regional tailoring houses and its designer labels, which draw on the country's labour skills and tailoring traditions with a level of seasonal styling but uncompromising quality. Here are a few notable names.

◗ Italian actor Marcello Mastroianni represented a confident menswear style that was distinctly Italian – as seen here in Fellini's classic movie *La Dolce Vita*.

Brioni

Brioni is one of Italy's most distinctive tailoring houses. Based in Rome, the gentleman's outfitter, founded in 1945, set out to distinguish itself from Savile Row and competing Italian houses by establishing its own artisanal workshop and manufacturing unit with skilled cutters and pressers offering a custom-made service. As Brioni's reputation spread so did its list of celebrity clients, including John Wayne, Gary Cooper, Henry Fonda and Sidney Poitier. Today Brioni sells ready-made and custom-made suits worldwide, upholding Italy's reputation for tailoring excellence.

Kiton

Kiton proudly represents a long tradition of Neapolitan tailoring, offering suits of exemplary cut and fit. The esteemed tailoring house works with some of the finest and lightest weights of fabrics that can be tailored to produce a custom-made or ready-made suit. A softly rounded shoulder is characteristic of a Kiton suit.

Caraceni

Founded in Rome in 1913 by Domenico Caraceni, the Caraceni label later expanded its operations to Milan and Paris. The tailoring house's 'bench bespoke' suits have gained respect and devotion from global clients who are prepared to pay a premium for the hand cutting and individual patterns made to fit clients' specifications. Exporting a tradition of Roman tailoring, Caraceni's famous clients have included Cary Grant, Humphrey Bogart and French fashion designer Yves St Laurent.

Belvest

Upholding a tradition of quality, craftsmanship and creative excellence, Venetian tailoring label Belvest exemplifies the allure of a 'made in Italy' label through its contemporary seasonal collections. From the outset, its founder Aldo Nicoletto aimed to supply the best ready-to-wear suits and tailored pieces. The company combines the highest standards of fabric selection and manufacturing techniques with hand finishing processes.

Ermengildo Zegna

This Italian label was founded in 1910 and quickly gained a reputation for producing fine wool suits. As the business grew and diversified, Zegna collaborated with international luxury design labels including Gucci and Yves St Laurent. Zegna is one of the largest buyers of extra-fine merino wool and continues to invest in textile technologies.

Giorgio Armani

Italian fashion designer Giorgio Armani is worthy of a special mention in the story and evolution of menswear. He reinvented popular tailoring in the 1980s when he famously removed excess weight and padding from tailored jackets; they became known as deconstructed jackets. His signature style is clean tailored lines and refined fabric choices, which also influences his women's collections. The Armani name commands respect and loyalty from media and clients across the world and exemplifies the virtues of Italian style for men.

Giorgio Armani epitomizes contemporary Italian style for men through his use of subtle fabric combinations and softly constructed tailoring.

American tailoring has been shaped by a combination of factors that, over time, have allowed it to evolve a distinct character of its own. European émigrés to the Americas brought tailoring skills and associated crafts primarily to urban centres such as New York City and Chicago. With a lack of alternatives, European clothing styles for men were widely promoted through early fashion publications and copied during the 19th and early 20th centuries. The introduction of standardized patterns and sizing systems coincided with the transformation of the tailoring industry from a handmade production system to mechanized, ready-made manufacturing. In response to supply and demand in the rapidly growing US economy, the new mass-produced menswear was sold through a growing network of chain retailers and gentlemen's outfitters, such as Brooks Brothers, to a receptive American public.

It is important to also recognize the significant influence of Hollywood movies from the 1920s onwards. Emerging screen idols such as Clark Gable, Gary Cooper and Fred Astaire transfixed audiences and set fashion and style trends that helped to define American tailoring. The key looks were copied and sold through America's vast retail outlets in the established pattern of ready-to-wear.

A word that is uniquely applied to one aspect of American tailoring is 'preppy', which embodies a respect for tradition, education and class or family ties. Despite the amalgam of influences that have shaped the early development of tailoring in the United States, an American sensibility emerged that is recognizable today. Described here are some notable names in the story of American tailoring.

Example of an American double-breasted drape suit, 1939, with broad padded shoulders and full-cut trousers with turn-ups (cuffs).

American preppy style as seen on a street in New York.

Icon: Cary Grant

Cary Grant is a Hollywood legend and menswear style icon. Born in England, he later moved to the United States where he projected a strong personal style, both on and off the screen, through his own interest in clothes and his sartorial collaborations with bespoke tailors including Savile Row tailors Kilgour and French & Stansbury. He manages to project a British–American style that embraces a British dress sensibility but with a relaxed attitude that is more American.

Brooks Brothers

Founded in 1818, retail institution Brooks Brothers is the oldest men's clothing chain in the United States. A Brooks Brothers tailored garment combines a European sensibility with a more relaxed American attitude. The classic Brooks Brothers suit is based on a two- or three-button sack jacket style with a natural shoulder line and centre-back vent worn with trousers that sit high on the hips, styled with or without front pleats, and held in place with braces (known as suspenders in the USA).

Typical fabrics include dark blue and grey pinstripes, fine flannels, herringbones and Prince of Wales check. Weights vary according to the season but include summer weight fabrics including silk mixes and cotton seersucker in fine stripes for men.

Brooks Brothers' famous male clients have included Clark Gable and Andy Warhol and numerous US presidents from Abraham Lincoln to Bill Clinton and Barack Obama. More recently the influential *Mad Men* series has seen customers flocking to Brooks Brothers for their trim-fitting men's suits.

American outfitters Brooks Brothers were commissioned to make some of the suits for the award-winning television series *Mad Men*.

Ralph Lauren

Ralph Lauren is synonymous with American style. The American designer has arguably done more to advance the perception and reputation of contemporary American tailoring than any other designer. The label's appeal comes from its aspirational lifestyle image, which is closely associated with a sense of heritage, tradition and refined elegance.

The Purple label, launched in 1994, represents Ralph Lauren's highest quality men's tailoring line and incorporates elements of traditional British styling. The label draws upon the expertise and craftsmanship of some of Europe's finest tailors and top-quality limited edition fabrics sourced from selected European mills. The result is a consistent aesthetic that continues to redefine a classically inspired American style. The company's Black label collection, introduced in 2005, added an Italian-inspired cut to its suits and tailored sports jackets, interpreted with a modern, American attitude.

Ralph Lauren's approach accommodates ease and drape into men's tailoring, so characteristic of American preferences; cuts include high armholes for greater movement and lightly padded sloped shoulders to complement a natural line.

Icon: Steve McQueen

King of cool Steve McQueen is a true style icon and Hollywood star who remains a source of inspiration to menswear designers and stylists. His cool persona and seemingly effortless looks have inspired men to imitate his style and clothing labels to reproduce his image and name under licence. His unique appeal crosses over between a sports-racing style, such as his appearance in the 1971 movie *Le Mans*, and his sartorial style, as in the 1968 movie *The Thomas Crown Affair*, when he wore a tailored three-piece suit. In spite of, or perhaps because of his early death, McQueen remains as an iconic influence for menswear.

Icon: Fred Astaire

Hollywood legend and famed American dancer on the screen and stage, most notably during the 1930s and 1940s, Fred Astaire was known for his impeccable dress sense and attention to detail. Astaire became associated with the formal attire of top hat, white tie and tails through his many films and made the look appear extremely elegant. Off screen he was no less elegant in his trademark sports jackets and trousers, often worn with a shirt and cravat. His personal style remains an inspiration to this day.

Oxxford Clothes

Founded in Chicago in 1916 by Jacob and Louis Weinberg, Oxxford Clothes is a discreet, European-inspired tailoring house that espouses a tradition of craftsmanship and hand tailoring not easily found in the United States. The company has dressed discerning gentlemen and public figures over the years including Clark Gable, Walt Disney and Joe DiMaggio. It continues to resist mass production methods in favour of training its own tailors and cutters. Using high-quality European fabrics Oxxford continues to define an American cut and fit with added service benefits. Under the motto 'American style. American made', Oxxford's 1220 collection is assuredly marketed as all American, drawing upon a style and heritage characterized by a certain ease and drape that spans business and social occasions.

J Press

Founded in New Haven, Connecticut, in 1902, J Press has come to represent American preppy style. Strongly associated with American east coast dressing, J Press continues to project a consistent visual aesthetic including the company's signature sack jackets, either as part of a suit or as a sports coat across a variety of soft tweed fabrics in subtle tones.

Among a select number of American men's outfitters, J Press offers off-the-peg jackets and suits as well as a made-to-measure service that exemplifies the virtues of natural and noble fibres combined with American finishing. It favours a traditional flat front trouser cut for gentlemen. The company also offers a full range of neck ties including regimental and club stripes as well as preppy bow ties and a range of gentlemen's accessories from collar stays to handkerchiefs. J Press's stated commitment to an Ivy League standard ensures its continuity as an American classic.

Men's shirts have been around for hundreds of years. Originally worn as an undergarment, the shirt was worn next to the skin and was only visible at its edges and openings.

Neck dressings evolved from neck ruffs to overlaid lace collars and later cravats. By the early 19th century full-cut shirts with high-standing collars complemented the stand-fall collar on coats and were dressed with a cravat or stock.

Differences between day and evening shirts evolved steadily during the 19th century; the amount of visible shirt front was formalized and largely determined by the cut of the waistcoat. Collars were detachable pieces that fastened to neckbands by buttons or studs. Collar shapes took on a significance that determined varying levels of formality. White dress shirts retained decorative detailing such as fine tucks, ruffled fronts or embroidery while formal daywear shirts were starched, with detachable collars and cuffs. Stiffened upright collars were worn with a necktie tied in a flat broad bow. Less formal day shirts began to feature patterns and stripes but also included detachable collars including a turn-down collar that formed the basis of the contemporary shirt collar. In 1871 Brown, Davis & Co, an English shirt-maker, registered the first full button-front shirt for men. Previously all shirts had been pulled on over the head.

White dress shirts with decorative detailing of fine tucks and ruffled fronts, as shown in this menswear illustration from the 1960s.

Custom-made shirts

Custom-made or bespoke shirts offer an alternative to ready-made shirts. Today they are largely the preserve of gentlemen and wealthy patrons who appreciate luxury. High-quality shirt-makers can be found in the world's fashion capitals: Paris, Milan, Rome and New York. London is also renowned for its shirt makers, who continue to produce English bespoke shirts worthy of a Savile Row suit.

◀ The classic white shirt, as featured in the Dior Homme A/W10 collection.

Collar shapes for daywear are subject to style variations, such as pin collars and button-downs.

Collars

The collar is one of the shirt's most distinctive features; it helps to define the character and style of the shirt. Detachable collars are generally reserved for formal evening wear in an upright or wing-tip collar shape as an alternative to a deep turn-down collar. Collar shapes for daywear are more subject to fashion trends and style variations but broadly include the following shapes.

Classic turn-down collar

Available in a variety of cuts with softly shaped collar tips. The depth of the collar should be in proportion to the collar band, so that a deep collar band requires a deep turn-down collar. Many well-made men's shirts are offered with removable collar bones on turn-down collars.

Cutaway collar

Also known as a spread collar, this style features an open, cut-away front. The cutaway collar is generally considered semi-formal and usually includes removable collar bones as standard.

Pin-collar

On a pin-collar the collar tips are visibly connected by a collar pin. The pin-collar usually has rounded tips and still includes contrast white collars. This style remains popular in the United States.

Tab collar

This is designed to be worn with a neck tie: a small tab is sewn into the front collar edge and helps to emphasize the knot of the tie. Popular in pinpoint oxfords.

Pointed collars

A style variation on the classic turn-down collar, pointed collars tend to respond to fashion cycles.

Button-down collar

This smart-casual collar style features a soft roll collar and is usually offered in oxford cottons.

Oxford button-down shirt

This shirt style is distinguished by a soft roll collar with buttoned collar tips. The button-down shirt was originally introduced by Brooks Brothers in the United States in 1896, inspired by the shirts of polo players. Not considered to be a formal dress shirt, the style usually includes a centre back box pleat and can be worn with or without a neck tie.

Trousers, more commonly referred to as pants in the US, are a staple item of clothing for men. Although closely associated with menswear, trousers and pants can no longer be described as exclusively 'male' following their assimilation into female wardrobes, particularly from the 1970s onwards. What we would commonly recognize as trousers today evolved from the pantaloon style of the early 19th century.

Pantaloons

Following the French Revolution and the abandonment of knee breeches for men came a new ankle-length style: pantaloons. To attain a 'smooth' appearance the pantaloons were held up with braces, while foot-straps, rather like riding stirrups, were attached at the hem and worn under the instep of the shoe. The close fit of pantaloons was consistent with the fashion for more fitted styles of clothing for men as well as the refinement of tailoring skills during the early 19th century. This also produced the anomaly of a male hour-glass silhouette during the 1820s, which briefly saw gentlemen wearing 'body belts', a male corset and thigh padding under their clothes to accentuate the fashionable narrow-waisted silhouette. By the mid-19th century, foot straps had largely disappeared from men's trousers, with a looser fit through the leg.

Variations

Striped and checked fabrics were introduced for daywear trousers and teamed with frock coats or high-buttoned sack jackets.

The introduction of pleats to the front of men's trousers offered additional comfort and ease. During the 1920s, a loose-fitting trouser style was introduced, called 'Oxford bags'. The trouser style was soon picked up by Ivy League students in the United States and appeared on the campuses of Yale and Harvard. Over the years, Oxford bags have been benchmarked against later versions of wide-leg trousers and the name has become more of a generic descriptor.

Pinstripe trousers with braces (suspenders) formed part of Vivienne Westwood's S/S10 menswear collection.

Creases and turn-ups

The 1880s saw the introduction of front creases on men's trousers. The creases were originally pressed from the knee down to the trouser hem. It is thought the practice was taken up to reduce the unsightly appearance of 'baggy' knees. By 1900, pressed creases on men's trousers had extended to the waist; within a decade, full-pressed trousers had become commonplace and remain so today.

Turn-ups, known as trouser cuffs in the United States, were introduced during the 19th century. Although the precise origins remain a matter of debate, some historians claim that turn-ups first appeared on men's cricket trousers at the Windsor cricket club in England during the 1860s when team members turned up their trouser hems by hand. King Edward VII was said to have turned up his trouser hems to protect them from the dirt and damp. After this royal endorsement turn-ups became a popular option for fashionable men and provided an option for some daywear trousers and sporting styles. Considered rather jaunty, they were not applied to evening wear or worn with morning coats or any form of formal wear.

Details

Men's trousers are defined by details, fabrics and finishing methods. All three should be duly considered when designing a pair of trousers. Criteria might include finishes such as linings. Half-lined fronts to the knee are preferable for comfort and provide slippage when sitting down or standing up. The finish around the waistband is a highly visible feature of a trouser and a usual mark of quality that many manufacturers have learned to exploit with their logos. However, the finish on the internal waistband serves a more crucial function for confirming a comfortable fit. Reinforcement of the seat seam is a discreet mark of quality, not immediately visible but evident when wearing a well-made pair of trousers. Well-finished pockets, buttonholes, seams, trouser hems and a split-back waistband to enable future adjustments provide additional quality indicators. The addition of pleats is largely a matter of personal taste, affecting the look and style of men's trousers; it is also influenced by fashion cycles. Inward facing pleats are considered more traditional than 'reverse pleats'; however, the latter can often create the appearance of flattening the stomach area and are more commonly seen on belted trousers.

Braces

Braces, known as 'suspenders' in the United States, were once an indispensable part of a man's wardrobe. Today they remain an important accessory among more sartorially inclined gentlemen. Braces should be sized to the individual, much like a shirt or pair of trousers. The advantages of well-fitting braces include their ability to hold trousers securely in place whilst emphasizing a flattering vertical line. They are most suited to trousers that are cut to the natural waist or high-waisted styles. Braces, unlike belts, also enable air to circulate between the shirt and waist band. Authentic braces are attached to trousers by means of buttons in an 'M' formation; that is, two buttons at the front and one at the centre back. Some tailors even advocate that the buttons should be visible at the front and concealed at the back.

American musician and producer Kanye West is equally well known for his personal style and attention to detail, as shown here in a preppy style.

Although the neck tie is a relative newcomer in the evolutionary journey of menswear, it has come to be associated with tradition and formality. During the early 19th century a variety of knots were introduced to complement the increasing diversity of shirt styles and their collar shapes. These included variations on the cravat and Ascot tie as well as a falling ruffle, called a jabot. Guides on how to tie different knots were published in catalogues and made available to men during the 19th century as the variety of neck ties increased and became increasingly de rigueur.

During the 1860s a longer scarf tie that was tied in a sailor's knot became fashionable for men, replacing the earlier crossover cravat styles for daywear. Flat, narrow bow ties in black or white became more associated with formal and evening wear. Bow ties also became an acceptable neck dressing for men wearing blazers. For formal daywear and 'Sunday best', Ascot ties were worn with white shirts, white collars and cuffs.

Selection of colourful men's neck ties. Silk foulard is traditionally used for neck ties and handkerchiefs.

Four-in-hand knot

During the 1890s a knot called the 'four in hand' became fashionable. Designed to be worn with a shirt and waistcoat and to expose the required number of visible studs on a man's shirt, the knot soon gained popular acceptance. It has been suggested that carriage drivers tied their horse reins with the four-in-hand knot, while others have linked it to how drivers wore their scarves. One possible origin is the adoption of the knot by members of the Four-in-Hand club in London, who quickly established the knot's popularity. Either way, the four-in-hand knot forms the basis of what most men would recognize as the standard knot today.

The Windsor knot and half-Windsor knot

The only real alternatives to the four-in-hand knot are the Windsor and half-Windsor knots, named after the late Duke of Windsor. Both knots require a substantial tie length and suppleness in order to be tied, representing a well-made tie in quality fabric to a discerning observer.

Illustrated guide to the three main neckties for men: the four-in-hand knot, Windsor knot and half-Windsor knot.

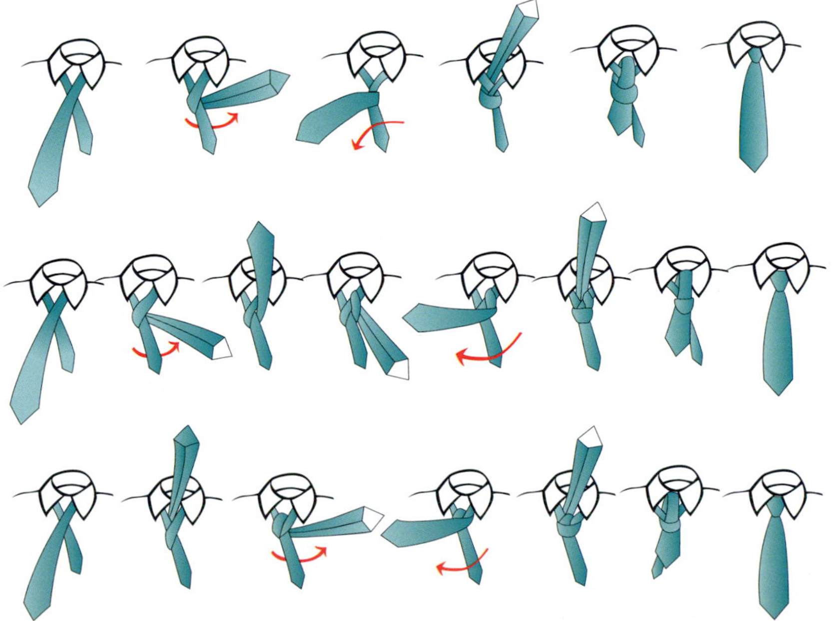

The bow tie

The bow tie has a distinctive character and offers an alternative to the neck tie. Informally called a 'dickie bow', the symmetrical neck dressing is no longer widely worn for daywear but has gained favour as part of the American preppy style. Bow ties have principally been consigned to men's evening wear and formal occasions. One reason for this is that most men were unable to tie them correctly, something that was supposed to have been remedied by the introduction of the ready-tied dickie bow; however, clip-on bow ties have never been fully accepted in polite circles where it is still considered gauche not to be able to tie a bow tie.

Regimental ties

The modern neck tie is largely associated with formality but has also come to represent a level of self expression, fashion and even humour. Regimental neck ties were introduced in the UK and have remained in style since the 1920s. The ties are characterized by their diagonal stripes, which originally signified membership of a distinct military regiment or section of the armed forces. British regimental ties began to cross over into a wide range of civilian adaptations as a generic striped club tie. Traditional English stripes run from the left shoulder to the right, whereas the stripes on American club ties run the opposite way, following the original Brooks Brothers style.

Neck dressings for men are closely associated with formality, occasion and status. Selection from A/W10 collection by Hardy Amies.

The modern neck tie

Forerunners of the modern neck tie were cut along the fabric's grain line and did not drape or wear well. In 1924 Jesse Langsdorf, a New York tie maker, identified a solution: cutting the tie on a 45 degree bias grain. Landsdorf also cut his ties in three pieces, making them more supple for knotting and draping. The innovative 'Landsdorf tie' was patented and sold worldwide and later refined and improved with the addition of the slipstitch to aid shape recovery. Most neck ties are cut and made in the same way today.

Historically, undergarments were concealed and relatively anonymous pieces worn next to the skin with the main purpose of providing a sanitary layer between the wearer and his outer garments. During the 20th century, however, and in parallel with the rise of branded sportswear, men's underwear came out of the closet and on to the pages of style magazines and advertising billboards. Adorned with designer names on waistbands and brand logos, the men's underwear market has undergone something of a marketing revolution since the 1980s and has played its part in presenting evolving ideals of male beauty and physical fitness.

Dolce and Gabbana are market leaders in underwear design; a highly competitive menswear sector. Dolce and Gabbana menswear A/W10.

The underwear revolution

Today's men's underwear market is big business and part of the branded menswear sector. Bold colours and name-branded waistbands, often worn to be visible as a component of casual wear, are a modern phenomenon of men's underwear styling and are readily available in a range of cuts, patterns, fabrics and fits from prominent American and European labels. In the modern evolution of men's underwear Calvin Klein is a notable brand leader. With a series of visually striking advertising and promotional campaigns the label has extended the commercial offer and fashionable appeal of men's underwear in a highly competitive menswear sector.

Undershirts (vests)

Combination sleeveless undershirts (vests) were widely worn by men until the mid-1930s. The war years saw American servicemen issued with undershirts with short sleeves, called T-shirts. Named because of their outline shape, T-shirts remained as undergarments during the war before entering the post-war male wardrobe in various forms including cotton jerseys, Aertex and ribbed cotton versions.

Technological and textile advances have extended the range of fit and fabric options including seamless garments, athletic elastane and cotton mixes as well as vests with thermal properties and a new generation of eco-friendly knitted fabrics in bamboo and soy fibres.

Colours and prints have largely been catered for through the style's rapid evolution into the ubiquitous male T-shirt.

As in tailoring, men's shoe-making has a well-established history and provenance. England and Italy both have strong traditions of making high-quality footwear for men. English firms still produce custom-made shoes from a last (the equivalent of a tailor's pattern). They are generally characterized by their formal, durable appearance and Goodyear welting (a strip of leather that is stitched to the insole and upper of the shoe and then stitched to the sole) making them well-suited to the demands of the British climate. Popular styles include Oxfords, brogues and Derby styles. Italian shoes are equally well-crafted but arise from a historical tradition of fashioning softer leathers. The United States also has its own shoe-making traditions that have been influenced by English and Italian shoemakers. Americans have embraced a variety of formal and less formal footwear, such as loafers and moccasins.

Brogues, also known as wing-tips, seen here with open lacing. Open-laced shoes are considered to be less formal than closed-laced shoes.

Oxford

Black Oxford shoes are among the most formal styles for men. Characterized by a toe cap seam and closed lacing, the shoe is relatively understated and restrained. Closed lacing means that the two sides of the upper are drawn together by laces that are sewn under the front part of the shoe, thereby closing over the tongue, which is sewn on beneath the lacing.

Legate

The legate shoe falls somewhere between an Oxford and a brogue. The toe cap is decorated with perforations across the seam line as well as along the seam joining the vamp (front section) with the quarter section (rear and side). Legate shoes are also a closed lacing style; a little less formal than an Oxford but more urbane than a brogue.

Brogue

Brogues are known as 'wing tips' in the US. They are characterized by their decorative perforations along the seams and curved top cap section. The distinctive, punched perforations of brogues can sometimes be seen on hybrid versions of Oxford and Derby styles.

'If you want to know the measure of a man look at the shoes he wears.'
Aristotle Onassis

Derby

A Derby shoe has open lacing, which means that the sides of the shoe are sewn on top of the front part. The tongue of the shoe is made with the same piece of leather as the vamp (front section) and the facings with the lacing holes that meet over the tongue.

Monk

Monks or monkstrap shoes are fastened with an off-centre buckle and strap. Popular in continental Europe, the style is considered more formal than some open-lace shoes and slip-on loafers but less formal than Oxfords and most closed-lacing shoes.

Loafer

Loafer broadly applies to a variety of men's 'slip-on' shoes. Tassel loafers are a popular British style, characterized by two decorative tassels at the front. In the United States penny loafers have remained popular since they first appeared during the 1930s. In Italy, loafers with a metal strap in the shape of a horse bit were made popular by Gucci and became a signature style for the Italian luxury goods label.

Dashing Tweeds

Who are the names behind the Dashing Tweeds label?

Dashing Tweeds was formed when I (Guy Hills) met Kirsty McDougall as she was graduating from the Royal College of Art. The philosophy behind the label is very easily summed up by the phrase 'Tweed for the 21st century'. Tweed is the original sportswear and, being made of wool, has tremendous properties and, of course, comes from a sustainable source. Tweeds were originally woven in natural colours and acted as camouflage in the country. Kirsty and I wanted to update this to work in an urban environment; instead of stalking, shooting or fishing, the main activity I undertake in London is cycling. With this in mind we started to weave some reflective threads into the tweeds to increase visibility at night, without looking garish during the day.

How have your different design backgrounds helped you define the label's style?

Kirsty and I both share a love of colour and the design integrity that weave gives you. There is a lot of printing around, which now, in the digital world, is very easy to do. The joy of weave is that little has really changed over the last hundred years and the new weave structures that Kirsty works out have a design credibility, which is very refreshing in this age. We both also enjoy the fun of dressing and many of our designs aim to bring a joy to people.

Where do you get your inspiration from?

I have worked with most of the tailors on Savile Row and researched their archives for inspiration. However, I am not interested in nostalgia as a design direction and so I use the classic style ideas as a starting point to move forward. Dashing Tweeds as a ready-to-wear label is all about modernity and creating clothes for the modern man. We are working on new silhouettes in the cuts, and on the weave side, Kirsty is working with a nano-technology lab, which we hope will provide totally new, functional fibres that we can weave into the wool matrix of tweed. So the inspiration is very much from observing modern life and thinking about the future.

Tell me about your interest in modern yarns and technologies

The interest in modern yarns and technologies is all about creating cloth and clothes for today's world. The view of the future in the 1970s was a white and shiny, squeaky clean place; the reality is that people want organic things with a heritage and ethical production but also want all the benefits of modern technology seamlessly integrated. This is exactly what we are trying to do with Dashing Tweeds. The clothes will be high performance but familiar.

Stowers Bespoke

How did you train as a tailor?

At 17 I joined a local tailors in Grays, Essex, and learned various basic skills, including managing and trimming the garments, mark stitching jacket bastes and cutting out trousers. I then moved on to Savile Row, moved into management, managing bespoke tailoring businesses and workshops, before starting Stowers Bespoke.

What for you, defines an English suit?

To me, an English suit fits the frame of the body in an effortless way. The waist should be shaped and it should have a good chest and shoulders; firmly constructed but not exaggerated. The style would be classic, but that is not so important as we are all individuals.

What makes a Stowers Bespoke suit distinctive?

Savile Row tailoring houses usually have a 'house style' or distinctive look and specialize in particular types of clothing. We prefer to operate in a completely different way from the other tailors, because I believe in giving our customers a wider choice. It's only possible because of our expertise, which is second to none. The opportunity for our customers to create their own personal design and style is limitless and exclusive to each client. Our skill set also enables us to produce both women's and men's tailored clothing and allows us to deliver the ultimate and complete wardrobe, from formal wear, casual pieces including bespoke jeans and fashion pieces and speciality items including shooting clothing, military uniforms and dress wear. By understanding and building long-term, close working relationships with our customers we are able deliver their exact requirements.

Who is the Stowers Bespoke customer?

Our customers are very diverse. Over the years we have designed and produced clothing for royalty. We have designed and produced clothing for a large number of films and actors including Jack Black, Ray Winstone, Josh Hartnett, Hugh Grant and Colin Firth and popstars such as Michael Jackson; we made the first military style uniform he wore.

Men's fashions all start as sports clothes and progress to the great occasions of state. The tail coat, which started out as a hunting coat, is just finishing such a journey. The track suit is just beginning one.

Angus McGill

3

Today it is sometimes difficult to imagine that men's sportswear wasn't always an option in a man's wardrobe. This chapter considers the transformation of men's sportswear from an early form of gentlemen's leisure wear to a youth-orientated global phenomenon that has become intrinsically linked to branding, technological developments, athletic footwear and street culture.

The impact and cult status of denim is also discussed, along with a short history of jeans and the proliferation of some distinctive, contemporary denim brands for further reference. There are two interviews with the designer-owners of a denim company and an eco sportswear label.

The origins of sportswear were in the 19th century and come from the established practice of dressing for a particular occasion or activity. This produced distinct modes of dress, such as the riding habit for horse riding. During the mid-19th century, however, with rapid industrialization in Europe and the United States, new forms of recreational activities were espoused by those who could afford them. Recreation was a luxury for most people and dressing for sport signified a social status and position that was reassuringly exclusive to the early patrons of sportswear.

From its early class-based manifestations, men's sportswear soon took on the role of promoting physical health and well being, which demanded suitable clothes for each activity or occasion. The reintroduction of the Olympic Games in 1894 heralded a new movement. It would take another 50 years for technological advances in textiles to develop what we would recognize today as active sportswear.

Variations of the sack coat as part of 19th century men's sportswear teamed with knickerbockers for hunting. Gazette of Fashion, 1855.

Graham Coxon, musician, in a tweed Norfolk jacket and knickerbockers by British firm Cordings.

Waxed jacket

The waxed cotton jacket is a country classic, designed for a variety of outdoor sporting activities. Waxed jackets are styled with a high level of functional detailing, such as double-entry zippers, bellows and concealed poacher's pockets, detachable hoods and press stud fastenings. Although designed for the country, waxed jackets have transferred their appeal to urban dwellers with a taste for the outdoors.

Traditional sports

Sports during the 19th and early 20th centuries were predominantly male, since women were considered too fragile or domestic to engage in competitive activities requiring physical prowess. Early men's sporting activities broadly covered a range of hunting, fishing and shooting pursuits, which saw the introduction of new clothing styles, such as the Norfolk jacket and knickerbockers.

The Norfolk was a popular style, originally designed as a shooting jacket for men in sturdy tweeds. It was also worn for cycling and helped to expand the range of British tweeds to the easier fitting sack coat as a form of early spectator sportswear. Knickerbockers became acceptable wear for golf and were frequently teamed up with a knitted sweater. Jodhpurs became established for riding and were worn with a close-fitting, high-buttoned riding jacket and a bowler (derby) hat.

Mackintosh raincoat

The mackintosh raincoat, abbreviated to a 'mac', is an authentic coat with an impressive heritage. It was founded in Scotland in 1823 by Charles Macintosh, who developed the process of applying rubber on to cotton twill fabric to make it waterproof. Seams were later sealed with tapes to avoid needle holes, thus ensuring the coat kept the wearer dry. The special combination of skilled craftsmanship and Mackintosh's exacting specifications have attracted international collaborations with luxury brands as well as commanding strong customer loyalty.

Fashion on the French ski slopes, in an engraving of 1934.

Polo shirt

The short sleeved cotton knit piqué shirt, with its button placket opening and soft collar, is a true sportswear classic. This ubiquitous item of menswear can be traced back to French tennis star René Lacoste's collaboration with a French knitwear manufacturing company in 1933. It was an instant success and was soon adopted by golf and polo players. As such, the style acquired its generic name as a polo shirt. A perennial preppy-style favourite, the polo shirt continues to retain its enduring appeal.

Twentieth-century pursuits

Sportswear during the first decade of the 20th century remained elegant, still largely maintaining the status quo of class distinctions. However, the years of warfare in Europe transformed previously held social attitudes. The more liberated 1920s and 30s witnessed new developments in the expanding wardrobe of men's sportswear, such as the innovative knit piqué cotton tennis shirt, credited to René Lacoste, as well as knitted jersey bathing shorts for swimming. Striped boating blazers and flannel trousers became acceptable sportswear attire.

Tweed and flannel combinations continued to cut a sporty dash among the more fashion-orientated men, representing a style of leisure wear that established itself as distinct from active sportswear.

The American influence

By the beginning of the 20th century, the United States had established a culture of informal dressing that was setting it apart from Europe, thanks to the forces of rapid industrialization, growing economy and a diverse climate. The USA had its own sporting interests in baseball and American football, which contributed to distinctly American expressions of men's sportswear style. Baseball jackets, colourful Hawaiian shirts and lumber jackets, with their bold oversized plaids, had no equivalents in the European tradition. Moreover, American men were more receptive to the sportswear notions of comfort and ease than their European counterparts. America assumed the spiritual mantle of sportswear, embracing it as its own. Since the second half of the 20th century sportswear has become synonymous with American style.

The arrival of the post-war teenage rebel and the enormous impact of Hollywood combined to accelerate the rise of sportswear, in turn influencing the landscape of menswear. Technological advances in textile manufacturing and finishing processes enabled sportswear to become a catalyst for change across many aspects of menswear.

Y3 is a collaboration between Adidas and Yohji Yamamoto; its launch in 2002 revolutionized the industry. Y3 A/W10 collection.

Baseball jacket

The classic baseball jacket is a statement of American style with a strong sportswear heritage. Closely linked to college varsity styles, baseball jackets have become popular items of sportswear spawning numerous branded and urban style imitations. The jacket style has evolved over decades but it is typically identified by a vibrant coloured body in boiled wool with contrast leather sleeves and an out-breast badge or sports logo, front fastened with press stud (snap) opening and trimmed with a stripe-knit banded collar and cuffs.

Bermuda shorts

The original Bermuda walking shorts were developed for British military servicemen who were posted to tropical and desert climates. Later the shorts acquired their association with the island of Bermuda during the Second World War, when the military shorts were copied for Bermudan civil employees. After the war the fabric range was expanded to include more lively colours and cool cottons, which established the style's enduring popularity.

⬤ Threadless is a specialist T-shirt company based in the USA. Members of the public are invited to submit their own designs, which are then put to a public vote by the Threadless online community and the selected prints are sold online. It's a good example of how the T-shirt continues to evolve and adapt with the times.

The rise of the T-shirt

In the Second World War, American servicemen were issued with undershirts called T-shirts because of their outline shape. After the war variations of the short-sleeved military T-shirt began to appear in army surplus stores and in the movies, where they were seen on a series of Hollywood male icons, such as Marlon Brando and James Dean in the 1950s and Paul Newman and Steve McQueen in the 1960s. The Hollywood stars did much to redefine the former undergarment into an item of clothing with sex appeal, which would go on to become the ubiquitous symbol of male youth.

T-shirts, sometimes called 'tees', are available across the sports and casual wear markets. They are a staple item of clothing in their original classic white or 'basic' form as well as being highly versatile, in common with denim jeans. Subject to fluctuations in fashion, the T-shirt has been printed on, embroidered, embossed, tie-dyed, appliquéd and generally customized by individual wearers over the years. T-shirts have become a perennial favourite of male peer groups and counter-culture dressing, representing an affiliation to a particular style, sport, brand or community as well as being an individual viewpoint as part of an outfit or 'look'. Not surprisingly, T-shirts have been adapted into a political item of dress, bearing slogans and arresting images, as well as becoming a tourist item, merging corporate interests with humour.

The T-shirt has become one of the most popular garments for men.

Denim occupies a unique position in the story of menswear. It transcends the seasonal vagaries of fashion and invites the wearer to apply his own style aesthetic. A pair of jeans is the most common yet personal item of clothing that most men own today.

Denim by Nudie Jeans, an ethical label based in Sweden. It uses organic cotton and ecological procedures for spinning, dyeing and finishing of the yarn.

A brief history of jeans

Denim jeans began life as work wear in the mid-19th-century Californian gold rush. According to legend, Levi Strauss, a 24-year-old German immigrant, left New York and headed to San Francisco with a small supply of dry goods from his brother's store, which he hoped to sell to the prospecting gold miners of the region. He took with him some heavy canvas, which he intended to sell for tents and wagon covers. When the miners expressed an interest in purchasing sturdy pants that would last under the rough wear of mining, Strauss identified a business opportunity and arranged for his canvas to be made into waist overalls. The new pants were well received by the miners but tended to chafe so, having improvised with the fabric, Strauss replaced the original canvas with a twill cotton fabric from France called 'serge de Nîmes' and had the fabric dyed blue with indigo. The hard-wearing blue fabric soon became known as denim and the waist overalls became known as blue jeans.

'I have often said that I wish I had invented blue jeans: the most spectacular, the most practical, the most relaxed and nonchalant. They have expression, modesty, sex appeal, simplicity – all I hope for in my clothes.'
Yves Saint Laurent

O Levi's collaboration with the French designer Jean-Paul Gaultier for S/S10 included reinterpretations of the American brand's classic styles and featured raw denim and red contrasting stitching.

Levi Strauss & Co

In 1873, Levi Strauss & Co began using the double arc stitch design on the back pockets as its signature mark. In the same year Strauss and a Nevada tailor called David Jacobs co-patented the process of putting copper rivets in the pants to strengthen the stress points during wear. The patent was acquired on 20 May 1873, a date that some historians consider to be the official birthday of blue jeans. Levi Strauss & Co sold its innovative new pants to working men and assigned them the number 501.

In 1886, the company added a leather patch with its two-horse brand design; belt loops were attached in 1922. The sewn red tab label was added to the left back pocket of Levi's jeans in 1936 as a means of differentiating them from other jeans brands. Concealed back pocket rivets were added in 1937. All the features became registered trademarks of Levi's. In 1954 zippers were added as an alternative to the rivet button fly.

In the beginning, sales were largely confined to manual workers in the western United States and the prairies, including farmers, truckers, railroad workers and factory workers. The war years interrupted usual production of the jeans; however, by the 1950s and 1960s Levi's had gained favour among post-war youth groups and subcultures and became famous for its best selling shrink-to-fit 501 jeans. In 1964 a pair of Levi's was added to the permanent collection of the Smithsonian Institution in Washington DC, assuring its cultural iconic status.

MOTO GUZZI

Icon: Marlon Brando

American acting legend and activist, Marlon Brando was famed in his youth for his good looks and method acting in a career that spanned over fifty years. No stranger to controversy during his life, Brando was dubbed a sex symbol by the popular media after his brooding performance in the 1951 movie *A Streetcar Named Desire* when he famously wore a close-fitting T-shirt. He gained further critical acclaim and notoriety in the 1953 movie *The Wild One* for his portrayal of a motor cycle rebel and gang leader in which he wore a leather jacket and denim jeans, greatly boosting the sales of both items at the time.

Denim mythology

It can be difficult to square up the mythology that has built up around denim jeans with authenticated facts. In the years following the California gold rush denim jeans gradually established themselves as practical work wear garments for North America's farmers and blue collar workers. During the 1930s it was said that 'dudes' from the east coast states who visited the former 'wild west' returned to the cities with a pair of jeans as a memento of their visit. The east coast visitors helped to introduce denim jeans to a receptive new audience but also helped to fuel the growing myth about blue jeans. The myth centred on the perceived associations of denim jeans with the American cowboy culture of the west. In reality, denim jeans were adopted by cowboys as late as the 1890s; however, they became inextricably linked to the spirit of adventure and freedom. The new jeans, with their refined cuts and style options, were taken up by American college students in the 1940s and the work wear garment began to take on a new youthful, masculine appeal. When screen and music stars including James Dean, Marlon Brando and Elvis Presley were seen wearing jeans in the 1950s, their cult status was confirmed.

Global phenomenon

The arrival of so-called 'designer jeans' marked a new stage in the global evolution of denim. Men's designer jeans were introduced in the late 1970s; there was huge market potential but the move represented unknown territory. The dilemma for the men's jeans market was that the notion of 'designer' flew in the face of their original appeal as an item of nonconformity and youthful expression. Within a few years and in response to burgeoning street styles that motivated individual customization, such as adding tears and bleaching the denim, manufacturers replicated the looks and re-marketed jeans to a more savvy public. In effect, designer jeans became streetwise. Premium denim brands today include some notable European and Japanese denim labels offering an array of cuts, fits and finishes.

AG-ed Vintage jeans

AG-ed Vintage jeans were developed by the American premium denim brand AG Adriano Goldschmied in an effort to create a distinct line of jeans with a vintage appeal and a modern silhouette. Applying a laundry technique that the company calls 'AG-ed,' the jeans imitate pre-worn vintage jeans. The number of washes is set to achieve the desired number of years the jeans will appear to have been worn.

Diesel jeans

Founded in 1978, Diesel is an Italian clothing brand with a significant denim collection, which has made it one of the leading men's jean brands. Its designs are skilfully communicated through youth-orientated multi-media channels of advertising and related communications. Diesel jeans are known for their high level of comfort and precise fit, making them one of the most sought-after brands.

Earnest Sewn jeans

Earnest Sewn is an American brand committed to producing only high-quality denim. It integrates the Japanese tradition of wabi-sabi (the beauty of things imperfect, modest and unconventional) with denim's considerable American heritage. Earnest Sewn's assembly processes are less about mass production and more about hand-crafted techniques; they offer a 'lived-in' look and ensure that each pair of their jeans is uniquely individual, a point that is celebrated in the wabi-sabi Japanese tradition.

Icon: David Beckham

International soccer player and English sports ambassador, David Beckham is equally well-known for his photogenic looks, product endorsements, charitable work and versatile dress style. He has become a global media personality and style trend setter with a devoted fan base. As husband to former Spice Girl and fashion entrepreneur Victoria Beckham, Beckham has appeared in numerous fashion photo shoots, including a well publicized campaign for Italian fashion designer Giorgio Armani, to promote the Emporio Armani men's underwear line. Beckham has also launched his own fragrance line and regularly appears in celebrity-watch blogs and international style publications.

⊙ Dutch brand G-Star produces fashionable denim styles for men and urban wear.

Evisu jeans

Evisu is a Japanese designer clothing company that produces premium denim wear using traditional, labour-intensive methods. The label's founding designer, Hidehiko Yamane, was trained as a tailor but his love for true vintage jeans led him to research authentic methods of production. Initial runs were very limited due to the high level of personal finishing and hand painting processes. Yamane's labour of love captured the imagination of denim collectors and an admiring Japanese public; inevitably the company underwent expansion but has managed to retain its status as a cult label.

G-Star jeans

G-Star is a Dutch clothing brand that was established in 1989 and became popular with students before expanding its appeal worldwide. The men's G-Star jeans collections offer a wide selection of denim styles and the company claims to have been among the first to introduce 'luxury denim for the streets'. Emphasizing the label's attention to proportion, craftsmanship and detailing, G-Star has now also introduced its RAW sustainable programme, which uses organic cotton and recycled fibre blends.

Kuyichi jeans

Despite its Japanese sounding name, Kuyichi is a European company. It has strong green credentials: founded by Solidaridad, a Dutch development organization, Kuyichi only uses organic cotton for its sustainably produced 'pure denim' collections. With its stated commitment to sustainability and traceable sources, Kuyichi produces an accomplished organic jeans collection for men and women with a stylish modern attitude and contemporary fit and wash finishes. In addition to promoting its organic jeans, the company is also exploring additional concepts of using recycled polyester, Tencel fibre, surplus denim and hemp.

PRPS jeans

PRPS is a luxury denim brand based in New York. PRPS's motto is 'Bruised, Never Broken' and the brand's priority has been to offer an authentic denim collection that places utility before fashion. PRPS uses African cotton and expert Japanese techniques of making unique and innovative jeans. The label's exacting standards and cool image have attracted the attention of celebrities such as David Beckham.

The history and evolution of men's active sportswear during the 20th century is inextricably linked with the development of synthetic fibres and technical finishes. Without the technological developments that led to the introduction of the first synthetic materials, with their easy-care properties and performance-enhancing finishes, active sportswear could not have advanced to the form of clothing and accessories that we know today.

In 1932, Willy Bogner, a celebrated German cross-country skier, founded a small business bearing his name, and started importing skis, accessories and knitted goods from Norway. As a professional skier Bogner was well placed to understand the requirements of skiing. In partnership with his wife Maria, he set about designing winter anoraks. Bogner established a reputation for combining functionality with a level of styling that raised the profile of the company and in 1937 introduced a silver letter 'B' to its zippers, in what is considered the first manifestation of sportswear branding. Bogner also began to diversify its business by creating sportswear styles for golf and a line of sports accessories.

German skier Willy Bogner at the opening ceremony of the 1936 Winter Olympic games. Bogner went on to found the active sports label that bears his name.
Getty Images / Getty / Images Sports

Freestyle skateboarder in urban casual street style.

485
480

Synthetic fibres

Hailed as a 'miracle fibre' when it was commercially introduced by Dupont in 1939, Nylon went on to become one of the most widely used synthetic polymers and a generic descriptor for synthetic materials during the second half of the 20th century. As the first truly synthesized fibre, Nylon surpassed the earlier man-made fibres, such as rayon and viscose (artificial silk), which entered commercial production in 1905. Nylon was synthesized from petrochemicals and established the basis for manufactured fibres, including acrylic, polyester and Spandex.

Synthetic fibres were used to create easy-care fabrics that were durable, practical and functional. During the late 1940s and 1950s clothing manufacturers began to identify opportunities for applying them to menswear. Ready-to-wear production systems, which were well established by the mid-20th century, were compatible with the new synthetic materials and were readily applied to active sportswear. Fibres such as elastane (better known by its trade names Lycra and Spandex) and Neoprene, developed by Dupont, have revolutionized active sportswear, most notably for swimwear and watersports gear. The advantages of combining synthetic fibres with natural fibres, such as polyesters with cottons and wools, were recognized by mainstream clothing brands.

Patagonia skiwear combines contemporary styling with technical performance and a commitment to environmental consciousness and social responsibility.

The use of synthetic materials in active sportswear has prompted questions about the sector's 'green' credentials. Sportswear brands such as Patagonia are leading the way with a commitment to corporate social responsibility and a mission statement that is backed up by championing environmental projects and joint ventures. Patagonia is one of the best examples of a company that produces technical sportswear to quality standards, incorporating a responsible sourcing policy that includes using recycled polyester, recycled nylon, organic cottons and chlorine-free wool without compromising the performance or style of its clothing lines.

Icon: Kobe Bryant

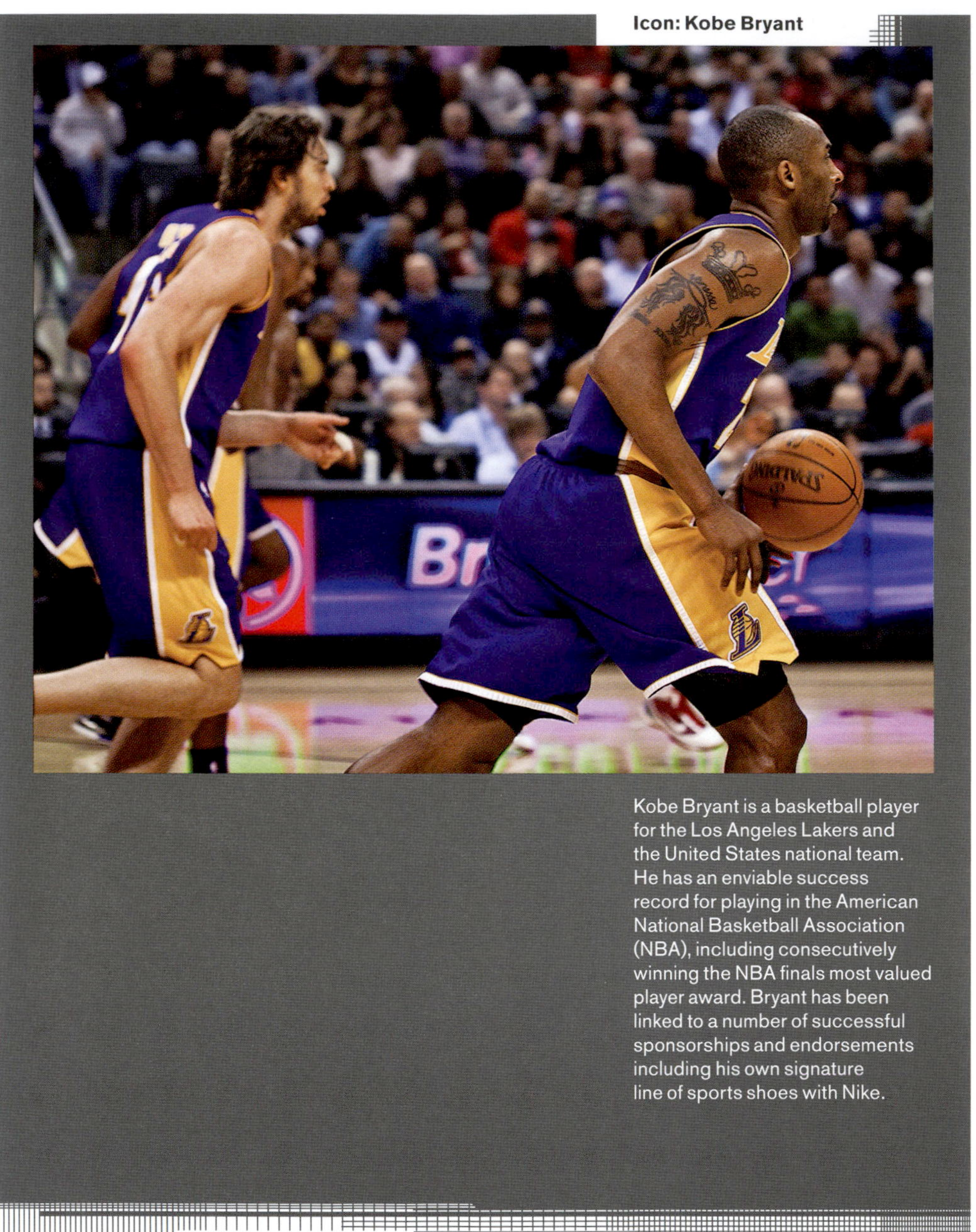

Kobe Bryant is a basketball player for the Los Angeles Lakers and the United States national team. He has an enviable success record for playing in the American National Basketball Association (NBA), including consecutively winning the NBA finals most valued player award. Bryant has been linked to a number of successful sponsorships and endorsements including his own signature line of sports shoes with Nike.

Global sportswear

The second half of the 20th century witnessed the transformation of active sportswear from clothing that was worn almost exclusively by professional athletes, to branded clothing and accessories worn by wider sections of society.

The impact of active sportswear on menswear during the closing decades of the 20th century was revolutionary. With its close associations to physical performance and health, sportswear would appeal to new generations of men who sought to break with the restrictive dress styles of their fathers and forefathers. Its post-war ascent coincided with the rise of the teenager and the phenomenon of youth-orientated pop culture across Europe and North America, the rapid advances of fibre technologies and the rise of media influences and new male role models across the fields of sports, music, film and television.

Adidas began to market its distinctive tracksuits, which were adorned with the company's three-stripe logo, as leisure wear during the 1960s. The fitness craze of the 1980s saw the tracksuit being reinvented as the 'shell suit'. These colourful, lightweight nylon jogging suits, originally popularized by professional athletes and made by reputable branded sportswear companies, crossed over to mainstream menswear. They fell out of favour in the 1990s having been over-exposed and copied by a variety of mass merchandisers. At the same time, new sportswear brands began to define themselves in a rapidly growing branded sportswear market, such as Nike, Reebok and Adidas.

Gore-Tex®

Gore-Tex® is a waterproof/breathable fabric that was developed in the United States during the late 1970s and patented as a waterproof laminate. Gore-Tex® fabrics are created by laminating the company's membrane system to high-performance fabrics which are sealed, usually with taped seams to eliminate leaks, and offer 100% waterproof protection. Successfully applied to co-branded active sportswear Gore-Tex® continues a tradition of performance fabric innovation that has expanded the active sportswear options for men.

Sneakers and trainers are among the most popular items of athletic footwear for men, transcending sports and urban wear.

Of course, active sportswear was never going to replace all modes of male dress and has had no real impact on formal wear but its widespread adoption has made it a potent force in menswear. Some sociologists and historians would argue that active sportswear has succeeded in replacing one uniform way of dressing with another. Certainly the growth and popularity of active sportswear has made it appear ubiquitous but its success has not entirely been the result of social and technological circumstances. Sportswear manufacturers and retailers have come to recognize the importance of ongoing technology investment and effective brand communication as a prerequisite for continued growth and success.

High-profile branding and signature logos have become an integral and indispensable part of men's active sportswear clothing and accessories. Without the association and kudos of the brand, it is difficult for a sportswear product to command its price or communicate its position in the marketplace. It is not surprising perhaps that the men's active sportswear sector represents a multi-billion dollar global industry that is driven by a competitive momentum to stay quite literally one step ahead of the competition: other active sportswear brands.

Converse All Star

Converse All Star trainers are also referred to as 'chucks', after the American basketball star Chuck Taylor who endorsed the style; it carries his signature on the iconic logo. These American shoes are a design classic, first produced in 1917 to appeal to the basketball market. The canvas trainers with rubberized souls and toe caps are available in a variety of colours as 'low tops' or 'high tops'.

The enduring popularity and nostalgic appeal of Converse continues to distinguish it from other brands and sporting shoe styles.

❍ Nike's 'swoosh' logo is one of the most recognizable brand logos in the world and adorns the company's extensive range of athletic footwear.

Nike

Nike is the largest commercial athletic shoes and active sportswear clothing brand in the world. The American company is identified by its distinctive 'swoosh' trademark, introduced in 1971, and its 'just do it' strap line. Combining technical specifications with aesthetic design, Nike has forged numerous collaborations and sponsorships with leading sportsmen. Foremost among these is former NBA basketball player Michael Jordan, who lent his name to Nike's Air Jordan athletic range with air cushioning technology. Nike's athletic shoes have crossed over into branded streetwear style and established a presence as part of hip hop culture. Nike has a series of retail concept stores called Niketown that incorporate sports, fitness, entertainment and new men's products as part of an enhanced shopping experience that continues to make it one of the most idiosyncratic brands in the world.

Reebok

Founded in 1895, the active sportswear company later rebranded itself Reebok in 1958, named after the African antelope, which was intended to help promote the company's passion for producing high-performance running shoes. Until the 1980s, Reebok's clientele had been elite athletes; indeed, when it launched on the US market in 1979 Reebok was the most expensive running shoe available. Reebok began to broaden its appeal by entering the commercial mainstream with the growth of fitness aerobics. Reebok continues to focus on innovative athletic shoes and has also developed collaborations with high-profile sportsmen and celebrities including the American rap artist Jay-Z and Formula One racing driver, Lewis Hamilton. The company recently teamed up with Italian fashion designer Giorgio Armani to produce the Reebok EA7 Collection of sports trainers and apparel combining European styling with Reebok sports technology.

➲ **Vibrant colours and synthetic materials have become characteristic of many active sportswear brands.**

Adidas

Adidas was founded by Adi Dassler in 1949; its trademark is three stripes, a design that Adi added to his running and football (soccer) shoes to make them stand out. Adidas's first and most distinctive shoe was the Samba: originally designed for frozen football pitches, the shoe quickly became the indoor-footballer's boot of choice. Adidas has continued to focus on research and development to design the ultimate shoes for track and field events. Perhaps the most iconic of Adidas's shoes is the Superstar. Introduced in 1969 as a low-top basketball shoe, its rubber 'toe box' became known as the 'Shell Toe'. This style soon transferred its appeal to urban sportswear and remains part of popular sports culture. Fans of Adidas have included American hip-hop group Run-DMC, who wrote the song My Adidas in 1986. Adidas has collaborated with top athletes including David Beckham, Zinedine Zidane and Haile Gebrselassie.

Athletic footwear commands strong brand loyalty among many menswear consumers and is closely aligned to fashion-conscious peer groups.

Puma

Founded in 1948, Puma is well regarded for its high-quality sports shoes and its innovative use of CELL technology, the first foam-free midsole. In 1985 a young Boris Becker won the Wimbledon tennis championships wearing Puma shoes. During the 1990s Puma launched its Mostro lifestyle shoe collections and consolidated its position as a premium sports lifestyle brand by collaborating with fashion designer Jil Sander. Puma has since collaborated with design luminaries Philippe Starck and Alexander McQueen. Fashion designer Hussein Chalayan's appointment as Puma's creative director is a further endorsement of the brand's style credentials, which remain at the forefront of the brand's appeal.

Gola

Founded in 1905 in Leicester, England, as a manufacturer of football boots, Gola became the first established British sports brand. During the 1960s and 70s the brand's reputation was enhanced when Gola shoes were endorsed by famous names in football, tennis, cricket and rugby. During this time Gola developed a range of sports bags, and, in a clever marketing strategy, the bags were given to team physiotherapists at matches so that when they ran on the pitch Gola's logo was seen. While the Gola bag became highly fashionable in the 1970s, the brand is equally well-known for its signature Harrier training shoe, which crossed over from sports personalities to become an established part of street style.

Despite the market dominance and celebrity marketing campaigns of the global brands, some niche brands are defining themselves in the athletic footwear market.

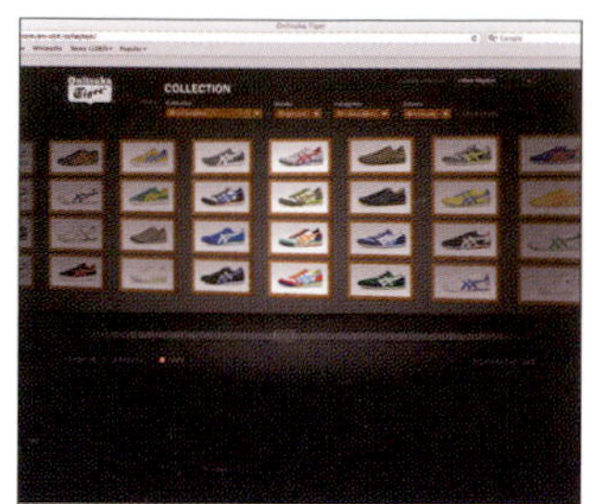

Onitsuka Tiger Mexico 66

Worn by the Japanese basketball team at the Mexico Olympics in 1966, the Mexico 66 represents the culmination of innovation and tradition developed by designer Kihachiro Onitsuka, who founded the company in Kobe, Japan, in 1949. The basketball-style shoe had a distinctive stripe design and a sole that incorporated Onitsuka's 'suction cup sole', inspired by the suckers on an octopus' tentacles. Since 1966, Onitsuka has developed his shoes in kimono fabrics, added sumi calligraphy and applied tsuri fabrications, using traditional Japanese design for an iconic, covetable retro-style shoe.

Veja

Since its launch in 2005, Veja has maintained its green credentials by producing trainers that have as little impact on the environment as possible. The brand uses organic and free-trade products, including organic cotton from Brazilian cooperatives, which is used for the shoe's canvas uppers, and natural latex from hevea trees in the Amazon for the sole. Veja's range of 'green sneakers' also includes the brand's ecological leather collection, which was launched in 2006 and only uses leather tanned with organic compounds.

Cruyff

When the legendary Dutch soccer star Johan Cruyff looked beyond what he saw as conventional sports footwear, he decided to develop a shoe that combined functionality with style. As a top sportsman, Cruyff was able to apply his unique understanding, collaborating with Italian designer Emilio Lazzarnin to add elements of style. The Dutch Olympic team wore Cruyff's at the 1988 games in Seoul, and the shoe styles have crossed over into streetwear. Key trainers within the range have included the Vanenburg, the Bergkamp DB 86, the Indoor Classic and the Recopa.

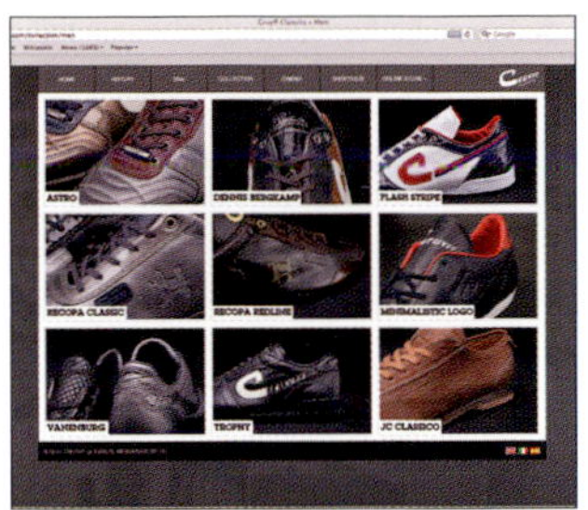

Feiyue

Feiyue literally means 'to fly' and 'to cross' in Chinese and translates as 'flying forward'. The brand has a distinctive heritage that dates back to the 1920s when the original sports shoe was first produced in Shanghai. Feiyue's original appeal was that it crossed all social levels in China and was even worn by martial arts instructors. The brand's provenance was rediscovered by Patrice Bastian and his French team who relaunched the Chinese brand and brought it to Europe in 2006. Working in partnership with the factory's owner in China, the French team has retained many of the original processes for an authentic 'retro' look, including the use of exclusive furnaces to model the vulcanized soles. The traditional, lightweight trainers have been blended with a French design sensibility to produce a covetable range of sneakers.

Sawa

More than just a pair of men's sneakers with a fancy logo, Sawa is a uniquely African brand that is working to invigorate and energize emerging economies in Africa. Sourced and manufactured entirely from the continent of Africa, Sawa represents a truly collaborative project between African nations that also encourages intra-African commerce. This means sourcing Nigerian leather, rubber from Egypt, Tunisian lace, packaging from South Africa and canvas from Cameroon, where the sneakers are made. Sawa has successfully positioned its shoes in the highly competitive sports shoes sector by identifying its unique provenance. This is resonating with consumers who buy the composite sneakers in high-end fashion boutiques in Europe, North America and Japan.

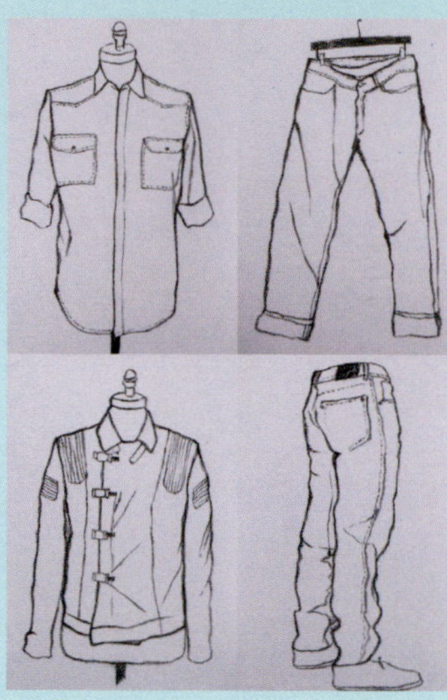

Where do you get your design inspiration from?

From almost anything that is devoid of pop culture or mass contamination from corporate dominance… a decayed brick in the street or a painting from a friend, inspiration requires having new eyes.

What is your motivation for promoting sustainability?

Our motivation to promote sustainability is simply the hope for a better tomorrow. It's been known now for decades that we will run out of almost everything we use today, so the system has to be redesigned. We all have to do our part.

How do you source your materials and production?

Living in Brooklyn and working in New York City makes it pretty easy to access suppliers and agents, whether it be at a trade show or showroom. New York is a huge magnet for almost everything related to the garment industry.

Who is the typical Mottainai customer?

One who understands the importance of environmental stewardship and values the feel and sensibility of high-quality products that are designed to wear-in as opposed to wear-out. Slow fashion…

What are your plans for the future?

Keep making clothes and try our best to make them available to those who need them the most.

Ijin

Ijin material is a highly original denim research product presented by English independent jeans-maker Philip Goss.

Tell me about your passion for denim.

Having already attained several tailoring accolades, whilst at St Martin's I nurtured a keen love of generic product types, such as military vintages and work wear denim. These became entwined with the traditions, hand finishing and personal interpretation of the classics, which tailoring permitted and encouraged. These passions were eventually applied to conceptual jeans making.

What does 'Ijin' refer to?

It is an old Japanese word, once used to define somebody as a stranger or an outsider. It can sometimes describe a person as a black sheep. The definition of *ijin* is the philosophy of the brand: Ijin material items purposely distort the rules of denim know-how, with clear intentions of presenting the classic indigo leg in a contemporary but alternative way. Ijin indigo is completely faithful to the methods of traditional jeans-making; however, the individualism of Ijin material is focused on the trademark 'half man' logo, which symbolizes the symmetrical folding techniques inherent in the way Ijin irregular products are actually cut.

Tell me about your slow denim production method.

Specialist slow-denim production specifically operates in an artisanal Italian workshop environment, focusing on hand-crafted limited editions and single item production runs. Here we concentrate on maximum human contact with the product by a limited amount of machinists. Ijin material is assembled by hand, with no mechanized help.

What type of denims do you work with?

Ijin operates with a keen eye on the authentic constructions of denim. The cloth type is chosen for its weave characteristic and not for its laundering properties. Worn from dry, Ijin fold-edge cut legs will render your own personal body map into the denim in a totally unique way, because of the cut and cloth combination. This process is defined as 'seasoning'. We also use various narrow loom denims for selected standard models; these are the most authentic denims. They are woven on vintage machines at a width of 27–29in and have a natural attribute for imperfections and irregularities.

In your professional view, what makes a great pair of men's jeans?

Effectively speaking jeans-making, like any art, is about care and consideration. Care about who makes your jeans. Men's premium jeans (specifically speaking) are less about fit and more about communication: the integral history of the maker should be apparent in the jeans; such as the self-edge type on standard Ijin items or the 'fold-edge' cut on the research line.

Tell me about your 'fold-edge' and 'wrap-leg' cutting techniques.

The highly specialist 'fold-edge' method I use cuts the garment open-legged in one piece, centred on the stronger warp thread of the cloth; similar to the concept of cutting out a paper chain man. Cut in this manner, the legs reach a near 45-degree bias point around the knee. (The warp of a traditional leg is found on the straight grain of the outseam. This is more about maximizing cloth consumption than the fit.) These legs will naturally mould to your shape, creating an inherent softness, even on an unwashed Japanese weave denim. The fold-edge cut is unique to Ijin material.

The 'wrap-leg' method involves cutting cloth with a dead straight but folded outer leg. Each leg is composed of one single piece of cloth and has a completely clean finish, run and fell inseam, as well as the trademark nonexistent outseam. Instead of an outseam, a knee-to-hip dart continues on to become the yoke, as it shapes across the back of the garment. These items are composed of only 10 key pattern pieces, including the three pockets; they are characterized by the fact that, when turned inside out, one cannot find any unfinished seams.

What are your future plans for the label?

Ijin has existed for six years as an independent in a multinational denim world, selling to the best stores in the world. The plan would be to keep it this way…

One should either be
a work of art,
or wear
a work of art.

Oscar Wilde

4

Designing menswear requires a set of skills that includes an appreciation for subtle and sometimes competing influences. This chapter is intended to support a critically informed approach to menswear design. It begins with research processes leading to the main principles and practices involved in designing menswear, including working with sketchbooks, communicating designs and following the critical path from an idea to the realization of a prototype sample. Influences for menswear design are identified for further reference while menswear drawing and presentation skills are also discussed. Interviews with designers provide additional insights into the evolving motivations and forces that contribute to the diverse menswear market.

Research for menswear design is a multifaceted process of making connections between design inspiration, gender roles, functionality and, ultimately, defining your customer or market.

Menswear has a rich history and heritage to draw from and can provide an abundant source of inspiration for menswear and womenswear designers. Today, broader themes such as work and leisure activities, uniformity versus nonconformity, sport, music and military influences as well as street styles all enrich contemporary menswear with creative tensions that can be tested and explored through design.

The process of designing menswear may take different forms but essentially follows a critical path from the conception of an idea to the conclusion of a final garment or range of garments, known as a collection. Menswear design is a commercial enterprise that operates across different business models and market levels. Its success may be measured in sales, yet good design has the ability to transcend commerciality by promoting integrity and offering originality. Designers should aim to achieve both of these attributes through a combination of creative thinking and an understanding of practical skills.

Inspiration boards can be a starting point for visual research.

Design research

Research involves identifying, collecting, analyzing and interpreting materials, processes or ideas, and it underpins the design process. Research explores the space between inspiration and a design outcome. Design research should harness 'inspiration' and channel it towards a design application or design solution. Effective research is really the bedrock of good design and is broadly categorized as either primary or secondary.

Primary research

Primary research for design refers to original sources or materials that have been identified, collected and synthesized by the designer. This might include, for example, drawings taken directly from studying a suit of armour in a museum or by taking original photographs of a sculpture to record and analyse its shape and form. The processes of identifying and collecting visual and written data are integral to primary research, which does not require an intermediary between the working designer and the original source.

Fabric swatches attached to menswear concept images, by Shefa Rahman.

Secondary research

Secondary research for design refers to the collection and synthesis of materials or data that have previously been published or made available to others. This might include trend forecasting information on colour palettes for menswear or seasonal fabric directions presented at a trade exhibition such as Pitti Immagine Uomo exhibition in Florence, Italy. Secondary research can be a useful way to access information. It is a mediated source of data that usually requires individual interpretation and analysis by the designer.

Utilizing a combination of primary and secondary sources of research is standard practice across many areas of the menswear design sector.

Line-up drawings by Harald Helgessen.

Inspiration

Although inspiration is often applauded as an essential part of design, it can become a nebulous agent if it is not productively channelled. Students will often seek inspiration first and then apply it to a theme. In the context of menswear design, however, identifying a theme or design problem first and seeking inspiration through a systematic research approach, incorporating primary and secondary sources, can also be a viable route.

In the context of menswear, design inspiration can include many aspects drawn from historical and contemporary cultures. Listed here are some sources of inspiration that may provide a starting point.

Historical garments

Investigating the origins and associations of menswear garments, such as the cut of 18th-century men's breeches or the functional detailing on military jackets or coats can be a revelation; it helps expand a designer's thinking outside contemporary points of reference. In turn this can lead to a process-led form of design research, where practical techniques are explored and tested in the studio and recorded in a sketchbook. Design detailing on garments is particularly important, often reflecting the subtlety of menswear. Thrift stores and flea markets can also provide opportunities to find 'authentic' original garments that can be analyzed and reinterpreted.

Digital collage illustrations by Harald Helgessen.

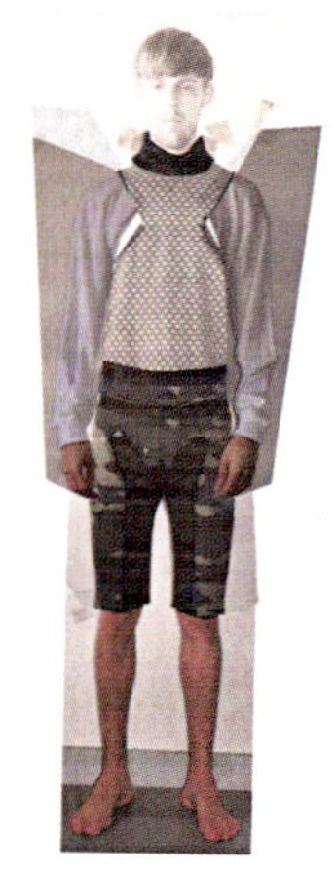

Fabrics

Fabric should always be integral to a menswear designer's inspiration and working processes. Collecting and testing yourself to recognize a wide range of fabrics is good practice and will serve you well. Menswear designers utilize fabrics in the production of first samples. The careful selection of a fabric can make the difference between a good design and a truly inspiring one. It is essential to understand fabric classifications, their properties and characteristics. In the context of design, fabrics should always inspire you.

Photography

The visual vocabulary of photography can provide a rich source of inspiration and ideas for menswear. The work of a portrait or documentary photographer, who may have captured intimate moments or diverse cultural perspectives, past or present, can often inspire and provide a starting point for the formation of an idea. Photography can also evoke strong moods and sensibilities that may set the tone for a concept board or collection. Drawing over a photograph in a sketchbook may reveal points of emphasis that can help to channel inspiration into a design focus.

Exhibitions and museums

Menswear, in common with all areas of fashion, sometimes needs to look outside its own discipline in order to refresh itself and generate new ideas. Aside from the enormous cultural value that visiting an exhibition or museum can offer, these public spaces can also be a huge source of inspiration to designers. They offer a wide range of subject content from diverse art exhibitions and permanent collections to special exhibitions that transcend social, cultural, historical and even political contexts. As with all inspiration it is important to be able to accommodate international perspectives.

Film, television and print media

While it could be said that film, television and print media are cultural barometers reflecting the current mood of society, they also influence and shape contemporary culture. Media influences are often 'picked-up' by trend-forecasting companies and fast fashion chains in equal measure. The media's portrayal and promotion of male icons, heroes and popular celebrities, including musicians and sporting personalities, continues to influence and inspire areas of menswear, both directly and indirectly.

Internet and digital communications

Rapidly advancing technologies, including the Internet and mobile communications, are inspiring some areas of menswear. The rise of user-generated visual content blogs and image-hosting websites, such as Flickr, are testimony to the Internet's direct impact and influence on menswear. Despite some protestations of a digital divide, there are many who find menswear-orientated sites a rich source of inspiration. This is particularly true for street style where bloggers are directly challenging once dominant print media formats and offering daily uploads.

Architecture

Architecture and interior design continue to be notable sources of design inspiration and remain recurrent favourites with many design students. It is perhaps because menswear is also concerned with three-dimensional shapes, balance, proportion and the selection of appropriate materials and finishes that architecture retains its enduring appeal. It is certainly capable of providing a rich source of inspiration that can be imported directly into sketches and tested in the design studio through processes such as pleats, folds and quilting.

Collection by Harald Helgessen.

◀ ▶ ▲ The youth-orientated appeal of street culture, with its rebellious tendencies, continues to make it a popular source of inspiration.

Travel

Other countries and cultures offer a huge source of inspiration and many menswear design companies encourage their designers to travel. Visits to international trade shows and exhibitions are quite common for design inspiration. This might also include visits to overseas retail stores or to gain broader cultural experiences where even the sights and sounds of another country or culture can inform a designer's appreciation for a market or prevalent style. Colour and fabric preferences for menswear can be quite distinctive according to location and can give rise to national characteristics.

Street culture

Menswear's close association with male peer groups and counter-culture dressing is well known and visually documented in many books and blogs. Street culture is a popular source of inspiration among many design students and has also come to inspire more established menswear labels as well as influencing men's styling. Its success over the years has led to a significant market in vintage menswear where authentic 'originals' have become covetable items and inspired reissues. However, the *raison d'être* of street culture is to remain outside the conventions of seasonal trends and formal collections.

Design development involves testing a design idea through a series of practical and skilled processes; it is the critical path from concept to realization of a first sample. Menswear designers work at the interface between creative practice and first sample manufacture for either mass production or custom-made design.

Design development requires a number of working relationships between menswear designers and an extended team that may include pattern makers, sample machinists, tailors, garment technologists, buyers and merchandisers as well as wholesalers and retailers. It is a team effort with the designer at its core. Effective design development considers all aspects of the design process leading towards the intended manufacturing outcome of a garment or range of garments. Some areas of menswear design such as tailoring are defined by specialized manufacturing processes.

For most menswear students design development usually starts with gathering and interpreting sources of inspiration. One of the most integral elements of design development for menswear is the ability to work with a sketchbook.

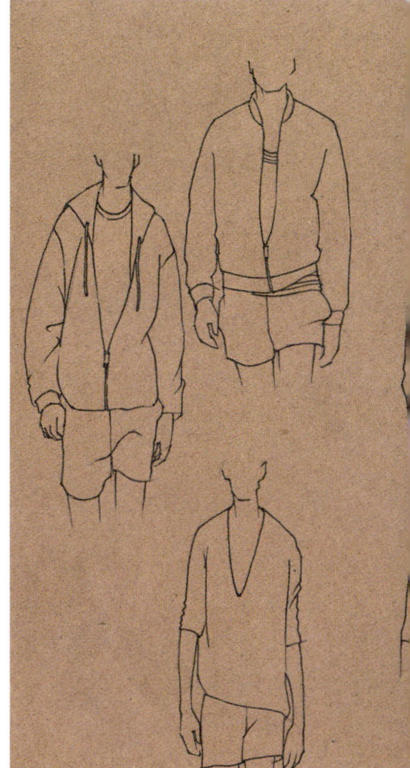

Sketchbooks

Sketchbooks are important tools for menswear designers. An effective sketchbook offers an evolving narrative of design thinking and studio practice that may include sketches; working drawings; fabric swatches; colour analysis; small-scale samples; technical information; primary images, such as photographs taken in the studio; secondary images, such as inspiration images; as well as evaluative notes and critical reflections.

Sketchbooks should enable fluency of thought and the opportunity to test and explore ideas in an unselfconscious way. The individual nature of a sketchbook should encourage all students to utilize it as a means of formulating an individual approach to menswear design through a combination of independent thinking, curiosity and observation, imagination and critical reflection.

Evolving over time, a sketchbook has the capacity to directly enhance the design process through sustained personal inquiry and investigation. At their best, sketchbooks become unique resources for designers with the capacity to support and clarify an individual approach to design development.

Linear working drawings by Brandon Graham.

Fabrics for menswear design

Fabric awareness is key to good design practice. Today's variety of fabrics and finishes can stimulate and enhance the creative process of menswear design. Selecting the 'right' fabric is a critical element of the design process.

When sourcing menswear fabrics it is worth asking yourself a series of questions:

- how does the fabric handle?
- what is the fabric suitable for?
- is the fabric made from natural fibres, man-made fibres or a combination of both? Fibre content will be a guide to fabric performance later.
- should the fabric be washed or dry-cleaned?
- does the fabric drape well?
- how is the fabric likely to sew?
- will the fabric shrink, fray or stretch?
- is the fabric finished to a performance specification? If so what will this mean in terms of working with it?

Some technical finishes can enhance the performance properties of a fabric but may require extra sewing and finishing skills. When selecting and designing with a chosen fabric in mind it is worth considering the following aspects in more detail.

Knowledge of fabrics and attention to detail is integral to menswear design.

Weave

The weave structure will give you an indication of a fabric's draping properties and how it is likely to sew. Recognizing the main weave formations, including plain weaves, twills, herringbones, hopsacks and dobby weaves, is also important in developing fabric awareness. You should start by examining both sides of the fabric to establish the right side. This can usually be determined by examining the selvedge. Some fabrics that are finished on both sides are classified as 'double-face' while others have a contrasting reverse side. Woven fabrics offer a wide choice for men and differ from knitted fabrics such as jersey.

Texture

Understanding texture begins with handling the fabric; choosing a fabric is a tactile experience. Does it have a nap or a pile? If so, it will have to be cut as a one-way fabric. Does it have a pattern or stripe? This will also affect the way in which you can match it and cut out the fabric.

Weight

It is good practice to lift up the approximate quantity of fabric that you intend to use to see how heavy or light it feels. You can also test the fabric's draping properties this way. Identifying and understanding fabric weights is another useful part of the design process.

Width

It is important to check the width of your chosen fabric before you buy it or cut it out, otherwise you could end up buying too much or too little for your design. Fabric widths can vary from around 90cm for shirtings up to 150cm for most suitings. Some linings are only available in narrow widths.

Finish

There are a variety of processes that are sometimes applied to individual fabrics, such as shower-proofing and water-repellent or brushed surfaces, starching or pre-shrunk finishes. Finishes will vary but can greatly affect the wear and handling properties of fabrics and should always be tested through a sample room or manufacturing unit before final use.

Colour

Fabric colours should always be viewed and compared in good natural light. Selecting the colour, tone or hue for a fabric is largely a matter of personal or customer choice. Colour selection is also a critical design function that will have a defining impact on the final design and may sometimes require colour matching.

Price

Fabric price should be considered in relation to costing functions and market requirements, especially for a collection or target customer. Menswear students are advised to compare the prices of comparable qualities by visiting retail competitors or direct wholesalers. There is little point in purchasing unnecessarily expensive fabrics; it is more important that the selected fabrics are of a consistent quality across an individual range or collection.

Cut and fit

Cut and fit acknowledge the fundamental principle that clothes need to address the human form, which moves and articulates in three dimensions. In menswear, cut and fit carry a particular resonance arising from the competing traditions of formal men's tailoring on the one hand and the more relaxed modes of casual sportswear on the other.

It is important to distinguish between the words cut and fit, since one does not automatically lead to the other. Cut may be used to describe all manner of clothing that does not actually fit. Cut also describes menswear in its broadest sense, from loose-fitting clothes to styles that are shaped to the body. The process of developing designs for menswear therefore requires an understanding of cut and fit and the relationship between them. While there is always room for testing and experimenting with cutting and fit variations, there is no real substitute for learning the skills through draping and flat pattern making.

Drawings showing line and cut of menswear collection by Brandon Graham.

The design issues associated with cut and fit also require consideration of the inherent differences between woven, knitted and stretch fabrics, all of which are used in contemporary menswear. Each variation possesses its own distinct properties, which should be considered through each stage of the design process from initial sketch or line drawing through to the formulation of a first prototype sample. This requires a technical understanding of how each fabric might respond to sewing and manufacture, as well as their appropriate end use.

A related issue to cut and fit is the ideal or desired body shape. Although this is affected by social, cultural and age restraints, menswear design is an evolving process where prevailing tastes and seasonal trends exert an influence. We have already noted that national characteristics and fitting preferences have led to cuts that distinguish one tailoring house from another. Ultimately, the designer's role should always be to make cut and fit contemporary and relevant.

Line and proportion

Proportion in menswear refers to the interrelationship between the component parts of an outfit. Line refers to the position of seams and darts, which provide the necessary shaping and overall visual definitions. It is possible to distinguish between three main lines on a garment. The first is the silhouette or outer line of a garment; this usually provides the first impression of the outfit and can be the result of either subtle shaping or pronounced emphasis. The second line refers to the style lines on a garment; the position of seam lines and darts, which can be visibly positioned, displaced or even concealed on the garment as part of a design. The third line refers to the detailing on a garment. In this regard menswear is notably characterized by an abundance of functional details; these include an array of pockets, closures, fastenings and additional utilitarian details, some of which have derived from military sources. Ultimately, all three lines of a garment contribute towards the overall design.

Menswear designers must also address the scale and proportion of the human figure. This is later tested through the pattern-making process but is initially evaluated and explored through the aesthetic process of design. Male proportions usually favour emphasizing the chest and shoulders. This has been a recurring feature of historical male dress and still provides an impetus for menswear designers today. Many designers test and explore the shoulder areas through combinations of padding, seaming, colour blocking and use of vertical lines. Collars and fastenings can also be utilized to help define the upper body lines and can give emphasis to the overall proportions of an outfit.

◐ ◑ **Computer-enhanced drawings of men's sportswear by Brandon Graham.**

Where curved lines are considered feminine and are usually associated with womenswear, angular lines are more often used for menswear to enhance the appearance of the male form. This can often be expressed through straighter seam lines and irregular surfaces and textures. Height is often tested and explored by menswear designers to extend the vertical form. This can be achieved through a number of processes and techniques, such as establishing vertical lines on the figure by using striped fabrics or introducing vertical seams or pleats.

While menswear is capable of accommodating different lines and proportions, the most enduring designs are thoughtfully considered and well balanced. The route to an intended design should also be tested through the process of creating a sample pattern.

Pattern making

Pattern making represents a critical step in the design process. It involves translating an idea from a technical drawing or sketch into a three-dimensional prototype or first sample. Flat pattern making requires precision and accuracy. It is usually based on standard measurements, a standardized sizing system where patterns are graded into classifications of sizes and used for ready-to-wear production. Bespoke or custom-made clothing for men also uses patterns but these are individually made for a client. You may not need to consider grading, but it is important to understand how to take measurements and relate these to patterns. Most menswear students work to standard sizes, such as a 40in chest and 32in waist.

The primary function of a block (known as a sloper in the US) is to provide a foundation shape from which a sample pattern can be developed. Choosing the correct pattern block should enable a designer to make the necessary adjustments without upsetting the overall balance of the pattern. Referring to a block where the line and fit have already been established should enable the pattern maker to concentrate on the styling and details of the design. A suitable block or foundation pattern should provide the desired line and basic fit requirements as well as all technical information, such as grain lines on the pattern pieces; seam allowances, which may vary across individual pattern pieces; and balance marks, including pattern notches for matching patterns.

Different types of pattern blocks

A standard block is the basic foundation pattern based on the system of standard measurements. It provides a basis for proportion and fit rather than style. Standard blocks are usually drafted as nett patterns, which means they do not have any seam allowances (turnings).

A production pattern is adapted from the standard men's block for the requirements of a manufacturing unit. It usually includes seam allowances to facilitate cutting and production techniques.

A tailoring block is a specially adapted pattern. Tailoring blocks usually accommodate some manipulative processes, such as collar shaping.

Pattern development

Students are often encouraged to combine flat pattern making with working directly on the stand, either to take further measurements or to test and compare the pattern with the dress stand. As a general principle, try to visualize the fit of a garment on a three-dimensional figure, even while working in two dimensions. Through visualization, pattern drafting becomes a more creative process, known as pattern designing. In this way creating a first pattern – a sample pattern – should be a fulfilling and rewarding experience that allows the foundation pattern or master draft to be changed as much or as little as required.

Toiles

A toile (known as a muslin in the US) is a three-dimensional prototype. Preparing a toile enables the designer to evaluate the accuracy and desired fit of the prepared pattern. All the pattern pieces must fit together before any attempt is made to cut into the fabric. The name 'toile' originates from a French word for a piece of cloth, usually linen; but it describes the prototype sample as much as the fabric, since toiles can be made out of a variety of qualities, constructions and weights.

A toile should always be made up in a similar weight and construction to the intended final sample. For example, if the intended final fabric is a jersey knit then the toile fabric should also be made from jersey; it should also be cut and assembled following the procedures for knitted fabrics, such as using a ballpoint needle and reinforcing knit seams with woven tape. Undyed calico is usually used for woven fabrics. The weight and handle of the calico should be considered in relation to the intended final fabric and assembled using the same sewing processes. If a garment is cut on the true bias (at a 45° angle to the grain line) then the toile should also be cut this way to accurately represent the final piece.

'Carelessness in dressing is moral suicide.'
Honoré de Balzac

Calico is suitable for marking on any alterations or style lines during a fitting review. It is important to judge a toile critically to avoid mistakes or fitting problems later. Alterations marked on to the calico toile can be transferred directly on to the patterns and adjusted later as necessary. Toiles may be viewed on a dress stand or on a live model. They can also be viewed in unison as part of a collection review or for a line-up to communicate an overall appearance.

It is good practice to document your toiles as you work in the studio. The images can be added to your sketchbook to assist your design development and will aid critical reflection of work-in-progress in readiness for the production of final samples.

Collection line-up sheet by Marlow A Larson.

Final samples

Final samples represent the culmination of the design process in the sample room or design studio. They should be successfully completed and resolved so that they can be presented to a buyer, press or private client. As part of a collection proposal, final samples should also communicate a coherent colour and fabric story that is consistent within the collection and appropriate for the intended market or client base. While the practice and notion of producing final samples may also apply to some bespoke tailors it is more usually used in the production of ready-to-wear menswear collections.

Collection line-up sheet by Marlow A Larson.

Range planning

Final samples are usually viewed as part of a collection proposal within a presented theme or merchandise category that is visually defined through a range plan. Range planning involves balancing practical and commercial considerations with aesthetic judgements. Since making samples takes time and costs money, it is worth considering the role and commercial value of each final sample within a collection. As with all collections, a menswear range can benefit from editing and merchandising to achieve the right product mix. Unless you are a specialist trouser maker, for example, there would be little advantage in offering a disproportionate number of trouser styles, merchandised across a choice of fabrics while offering only a few jackets or tops. The result would be an imbalanced collection.

While a collection should by its very nature offer the customer choice, it should also be balanced and communicate a cohesive identity. The identity of a collection is often expressed through a design theme and the final samples should also offer a balance between the prevailing silhouettes, fabrics and styling features to present a new and contemporary look. Fittings should be consistent within the collection so that a jacket can be worn with trousers or a topcoat or parka style in the same size. For menswear students the final samples should be complemented with a portfolio of work that includes photographs and illustrations.

As a guide, male fashion figures are drawn with less exaggerated proportions than female figures. While a man's body is broader than a woman's the vertical proportions are quite similar except for the muscle structure, which is significantly more defined in a man. The torso is drawn slightly longer than for a woman while the chest is broader and the waist is larger and positioned a little lower. Height may be added to the legs rather than the neck. The shoulders should be broad with a thick neck. Hands, knees and feet are all drawn quite prominently.

Drawing men

When drawing from life it is essential to study the pose before you begin to draw, remembering that there is no substitute for analyzing the structural elements of each pose. Start by sketching the male figure in a relaxed pose. Transferring the weight on to one leg is a characteristic fashion pose. This allows a 'flow' through the body. In order for the figure to appear balanced, however, the axial line (also known as the balance line) should appear to drop vertically from the base of the neck to the heel of the supporting foot. When drawing a standing figure, the axial line determines the weight distribution and balance of the male figure. The balance point falls between the legs when the weight is evenly distributed. Remember that the supporting leg isn't drawn with the same amount of curvature as for a woman since a man's pelvis is less pronounced.

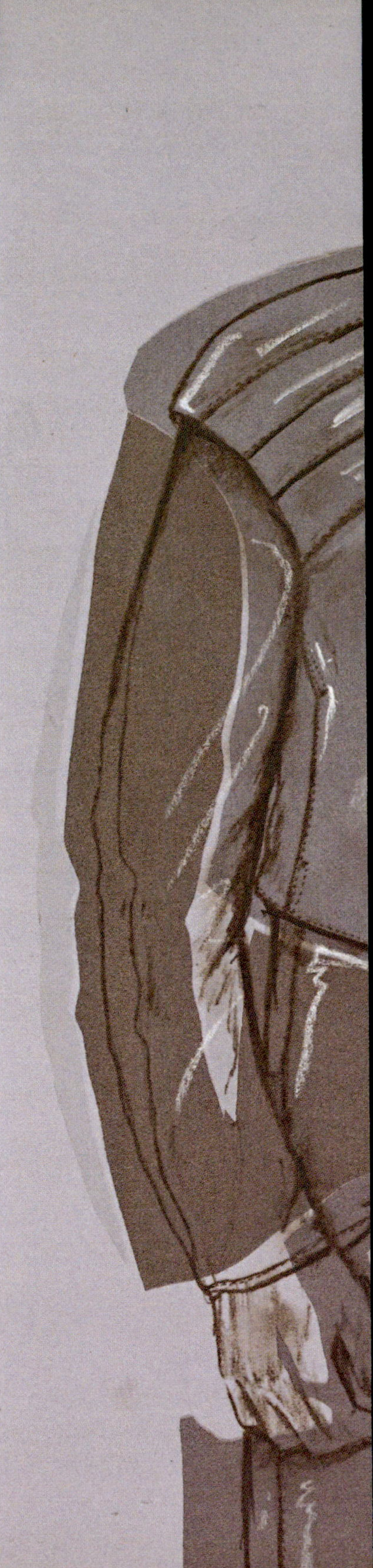

Illustration by Crystal McFarlane.

When drawing the male figure the slant of the shoulder and pelvis should be less exaggerated than for a woman. Make sure that the shoulders and upper chest are always broader than the hips, to create an angular torso shape. Realistic facial and apparel details are more typical of menswear illustrations. Fabric rendering is also important and should take account of the variety of fabrics that make up contemporary menswear. When an illustration requires a more mature man, additional bulk may be added to the torso and shoulders.

Because of the subtlety of some aspects of men's clothing and because the poses are less stylized than for womenswear, menswear illustrators need to develop an eye for capturing fit and detail. Representing the shape of a shoulder line or the width of a lapel, for example, are significant when illustrating a man's suit.

Composition and visual layout

The composition and visual layout of artwork for menswear should be carefully considered in order to clearly communicate the information. The artwork may be artistic, such as an illustration, or more technical, such as menswear flats. It is always good practice to visually link your artwork boards across a project.

The visual elements on menswear presentation boards are usually a combination of drawings, fabric swatches, photographs, trimmings and written text. The arrangement of these elements on the page or presentation board is governed by the principles of the positive image and negative space. The positive image refers directly to the subject. In menswear design this might be the male fashion figure or a garment 'flat'. Negative space refers to the space around and between the subjects. Negative space is a vital element in a visual presentation; the relationship between the positive image and negative space constitutes the layout and determines the effectiveness of the final composition.

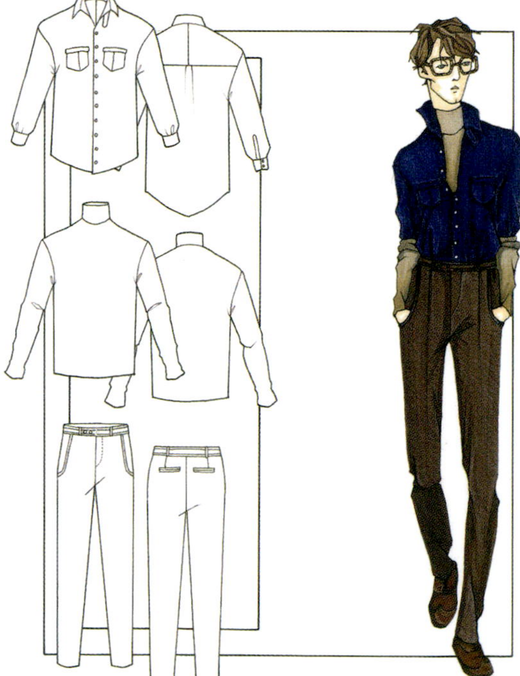

Design boards by Marlow A Larson.

◀ ▼ **Line-up drawings by Mengjie Di.**

The layout of a successful menswear presentation considers the placement of all the visual elements in order to capture attention and direct the viewer's eye over the presentation. Trimming fabrics, adding inspirational background images and positioning flats with a figurative illustration are all effective techniques. Before the arrival of digital media rough drafts were prepared by hand. Today most presentation boards are prepared digitally or converted to digital formats. This has transformed the process of editing and preparing presentations through digital layers; presentations may then be edited and formatted.

Studying the elements of visual design and understanding how they work together on a presentation board or across a project will help you develop and improve your compositions. Planning a composition and designing the layout should always be prioritized and considered against the context and purpose of the artwork.

Collage and mixed media

Collage and mixed media have become popular choices with many illustrators. Collage and mixed media are not a replacement for drawing but can extend the range and application of hand rendering. Collage is an effective way of creating impact in an illustration or visual composition. Originally adopted by artists as a process of assembling different forms of mixed media to create new work, collage offers almost unlimited scope to illustrators; media such as photographs, scanned fabrics, textures and surfaces and found objects can all be used.

Collage for menswear is popular because it can be used to create visually engaging compositions outside the usual conventions of drawing media. Hand-made collages also encompass particular tactile and textural qualities that can add depth to the final illustration. Used in combination with digital software formats such as Photoshop, collage is a highly versatile media. Ongoing advances in digital graphics software have enabled fashion illustrators to explore the scope and appeal of collage; today many designers and fashion illustrators combine formats for a contemporary drawing style.

Developing collage or mixed media illustrations for menswear is a creative process that encourages a high level of personal expression. As with most approaches to creating artwork, this multifaceted approach to media is enhanced through exploration and practice, which can produce some unexpected results whilst encouraging inventiveness, curiosity and compositional skills.

Mixed media collage boards by Shefa Rahman.

Mixed media collage boards by Shefa Rahman.

Menswear students will require a portfolio of artwork to gain employment as a designer. A menswear portfolio should provide a coherent visual statement of individual achievement and indicate future ambition.

Portfolio pages by Mengjie Di.

Content and organization

Content and organization are key to a successful portfolio. A menswear portfolio should demonstrate individual strengths and abilities. While four or five accomplished projects are usually enough to represent your work, the ability to edit work is essential. Menswear portfolios may vary in style and format, so reviewing content and organization is about focusing a portfolio for a defined market or target audience.

The content of a menswear portfolio is likely to include a selection of artwork and presentation boards themed by project. Each project should open with a mood board or concept board to introduce the context and source of inspiration for the designs. Colours and fabrics should be given careful consideration across all project presentations. Flats are particularly important for ready-to-wear menswear and should feature in all sportswear projects. Illustration offers scope but should always be appropriate to the target market.

In addition to a physical portfolio case of selected artwork, some menswear designers are using digital e-portfolios to present and customize their work. Blogs and image-hosting websites such as Flickr and Issuu now offer new platforms for menswear designers to communicate their work to wider audiences.

Giles Price

Please outline your current job and your career path

I am currently working on a female mma (cage fighting) reportage and film documentary project, as well as a documentary for the British Fashion Council. I see the mixing of my stills approach and film as the natural growth of my work.

How would you describe your photography style?

It is graphic and raw visually, but within that has a poetic quality. I like the synergy of the two. I always try to engage with the context of what I am showing and why, be that playing to it or against it.

What or who inspires you?

Reinhold Messner, Ueli Steck, John Gray, James Lovelock, Adam Curtis. A few explorers of the physical and cerebral, who keep pushing forward.

Tell me about your 1234 revellers portraits

The 1234 was a project I made with the organizers of the 1234 Shoreditch Festival in London, UK. We shot the festival goers over the course of the day in a mobile studio on site.

How does photographing men differ from how you might photograph women?

I shoot everyone the same way, which gets me into problems when shooting women commercially. Cultural notions, of what is beautiful in regard to the representation of women, are so small now that anything outside of them is not even considered; retouching has rubbed out the life and beauty of imperfections and expression for a heavily stylized dystopia of plastic falseness and PR-generated image branding myths. It is boring and becoming more benign and of no help to viewers. Saying that, it may be starting to change – we shall see.

What would you consider has been your greatest photographic achievement to date?

My best achievements so far have been the Old Guard: the last World War 1 veterans and Johnson Beharry VC; both of these projects hit historically lasting moments, which can never be repeated.

When was the Peter Jensen menswear label established and where do you present your collections?

The business was launched 10 years ago and has always been based in London. After leaving college Peter designed menswear under his own name working with an Italian agent, Eo Bocci. The first menswear show was in Paris. From A/W01 onwards Peter worked independently, producing both men's and women's collections. Shows in London and Copenhagen followed, before MAC cosmetics invited Peter Jensen to present in New York.

How would you describe the label's menswear style?

It's about evolving classic pieces from one season to the next. We use a lot of colour and print with a quirky sensibility that has an element of humour in it. This is partly achieved by styling, where we combine unexpected colours, details and prints.

Where do you get your inspiration from?

The menswear label is designed before the womenswear collection but the womenswear pieces are generally more directional and influence some of the menswear looks. We do have references for the menswear collections that include art photographers, individual style and everyday sources of inspiration.

How do you design and update your menswear collections?

We're always thinking about what we want to wear but also about what we think is right for the brand image and what has been popular in previous collections.

Who is the classic Peter Jensen menswear customer?

I think the perception of the menswear label is quite young because of the playful elements in the collections but it should also appeal to an older customer too.

What are your plans for the future of the label?

We're constantly trying to refine what we do, which is an ongoing process. Next year we will have been in business 10 years and we're working on a retrospective book; it's a really interesting process.

Menswear exists within a framework of competing contexts and influences. An informed view of contemporary menswear requires an acknowledgement and basic understanding of its historical evolution including associations with utility and military dressing. The rules and subtleties of male dressing have provided some historical flash points and creative tensions between formal aspects of menswear and youthful, more rebellious expressions.

Although menswear is affected and influenced by a mix of social and cultural forces, it also gains impetus from addressing and confronting issues and debates surrounding gender, status and identity. Designing menswear requires the ability to critically identify, select, evaluate and interpret these factors; linking an idea to a set of processes that takes account of fabric, line, proportion and detailing. Contemporary menswear design continues to evolve, as illustrated through the interviews with designers in this book. Their individual practices reveal personal approaches and styles that enable menswear to continue its evolutionary journey.

I hope this book has stimulated your interest and will inspire you to extend your critical awareness of menswear design.

A/W09 menswear collection by Thom Browne.

Anderson, Richard
Bespoke:
Savile Row Ripped and Smoothed
Simon & Schuster Ltd (2009)

Blackman, Cally
100 Years of Menswear
Laurence King (2009)

Boston, Lloyd
Men of Color:
Fashion, History, Fundamentals
Workman Publishing (reprint edition 2001)

Cicolini, Alice
The New English Dandy
Thames & Hudson (2007)

Davies, Hywel
Modern Menswear
Laurence King (2008)

Flusser, Alan
Dressing the Man
Harper Collins (2003)

Hayashida, Teruyoshi
Take Ivy
Powerhouse Books (reprint edition 2010)

Marsh, Graham and Gaul, JP
The Ivy Look:
Classic American Clothing –
An Illustrated Pocket Guide
Frances Lincoln (2010)

Musgrave, Eric
Sharp Suits
Pavilion (2009)

Schuman, Scott
The Sartorialist
Pengiun (2009)

Sherwood, James
Bespoke:
The Men's Style of Savile Row
Rizzoli International Publications (2010)

Sherwood, James
Savile Row:
The Master Tailors of British Bespoke
Thames & Hudson (2010)

Sherwood, James
The London Cut:
Savile Row Bespoke Tailoring
Marsilio (2007)

Tamagni, Daniele
Gentlemen of Bacongo
Trolley (2009)

Wayne, Chidy
Essential Fashion Illustration:
Men
Rockport Publishers (2009)

Trade exhibitions

Bread & Butter, Germany
breadandbutter.com
Trade fair for contemporary casual, streetwear, denim and sportswear

Idea Biella, Italy
ideabiella.it
Seasonal presentation of top-range men's fabrics

Label, UK
purelondon.com
Exhibition and buying fair for young branded fashion

MAGIC, Las Vegas, USA
magiconline.com
USA men's apparel and accessory trade show

Milano Moda Uomo, Italy
cameramoda.it/mmu
Presentation of men's ready-to-wear designer collections

Moda Menswear, UK
moda-uk.co.uk
UK tradeshow for contemporary and mainstream menswear

Mode Masculine, France
modeaparis.com
Presentation of men's ready-to-wear designer collections

MRket, New York City and Las Vegas, USA
mrketshow.com
Exclusive show for the menswear industry

Pitti Uomo, Italy
pittimmagine.com/it/fiere/uomo
Premium menswear trade show

Premiere Vision, France
premierevision.fr
Seasonal presentation of European and international fabrics for men and women

Blogs

acontinuouslean.com

asuitablewardrobe.dynend.com

designerman-whatisawtoday.blogspot.com

englishcut.com

facehunter.blogspot.com

ivy-style.com

sleevehead.blogspot.com

theimpossiblecool.tumblr.com

thesartorialist.blogspot.com

thetrad.blogspot.com

youngmanoldman.blogspot.com

Magazines and journals

AnOther Man

Dazed and Confused

Details

DNR News

Drapers

Esquire

GQ

i-D

L'Uomo Vogue

Pop

Tank

10

Compiled by Indexing Specialists (UK) Ltd

I would like to thank all the contributors who generously provided original material for this book and to those who agreed to be interviewed. In alphabetical order:
Lou Dalton
Mengjie Di
Russ Gater
Philip Goss
Brandon Graham
Harald Helgesen
Guy Hills
Marlow A Larson
Robert Lindo
Luke McCann
Kirsty McDougall
Crystal McFarlane
Giles Price
Shefa Rahman
Daniel Savory
Ray Stowers and
Gerard Wilson.

Special thanks also to:
Lucy Barker
Dahren Davey
Ray Hammett
Sachiko Honda
Cecilia Langemar
Robert Leach and
Leonie Taylor
for their additional help and assistance.

Thank you to everyone at AVA books, especially Rachel Netherwood, and to John McGill.

Picture credits

p 015 courtesy of The Art Archive
p 025 courtesy of The Art Archive / Musée des Arts Décoratifs Paris / Alfredo Dagli Orti
p 026 courtesy of Gloverall
p 028 (bottom) courtesy of Vintage Whistles
p 030 courtesy of The Art Archive / Museo de las Culturas Oaxaca / Gianni Dagli Orti
p 031 courtesy of Bryn Mawr College Library
p 035 courtesy of R Bamber / Rex Features
p 037 courtesy of Warner Bros / The Kobal Collection / McCarty, Floyd
p 038 courtesy of 20th Century Fox / The Kobal Collection / Morton, Merrick
p 039 courtesy of Everett Collection / Rex Features
p 041 courtesy of 20th Century Fox / The Kobal Collection
p 042 (top) courtesy of Michael Webb / Hulton Archive / Getty Images
p 043 courtesy of David McEnery / Rex Features
p 044 (top) courtesy of Terry Spencer © Cara Spencer / Museum of London
p 044 (bottom) courtesy of Baracuta
p 046 courtesy of Roger Bamber / Rex Features
p 047 (top) courtesy of Dave Hogan / Hulton Archive / Getty Images
p 047 (bottom) courtesy of Schott
p 048 courtesy of Richard Young / Rex Features
pp 050–051 courtesy of Heritage Research
pp 052–053 courtesy of Lou Dalton
p 058 courtesy of Anderson & Sheppard
p 059 (top) courtesy of Cordings
p 062 © Daniele Tamagni courtesy of Michael Hoppen Contemporary
p 070 courtesy of Anderson & Sheppard
p 073 courtesy of Richard James
p 075 courtesy of Express / Archive Photos / Getty Images
p 077 courtesy of Riama-Pathe / The Kobal Collection
p 081 courtesy of Eddie Newton and Stylesight
p 083 courtesy of AMC / The Kobal Collection
p 085 courtesy of United Artists / The Kobal Collection
p 086 courtesy of MGM / The Kobal Collection / Bull, Clarence Sinclair
pp 104–105 courtesy of Dashing Tweeds
pp 106–107 courtesy of Stowers Bespoke
p 111 courtesy of Cordings
p 112 courtesy of Barbour
p 113 courtesy of Mackintosh
p 114 courtesy of The Art Archive / Private Collection / Marc Charmet
p 119 courtesy of Out of Print
p 120 courtesy of Nudie Jeans
p 124 courtesy of Warner Bros / The Kobal Collection / Engstead, John
p 130 courtesy of Getty Images / Getty Images Sport
p 132 courtesy of Patagonia
p 135 courtesy of Gore-Tex®
p 137 courtesy of Peter Miszuk
pp 144–145 courtesy of Mottainai
pp 146–149 courtesy of Ijin
pp 182–183 courtesy of Giles Price
pp 184–185 courtesy of Peter Jensen
pp 007, 029, 034, 042 (bottom), 066, 079, 089, 093, 098, 100, 116, 122–123 courtesy of Catwalking.com
pp 024, 095, 160–161 courtesy of Stylesight.
Stylesight (www.stylesight.com) is the leading online provider of trend content, tools and technology for creative professionals in the style and design industries. Founded in 2003, Stylesight targets professionals involved in the creative design and product development processes, assisting them through its unique Creative Platform with content and tools that make the design journey more efficient, less costly, faster and accurate.

BASICS FASHION

Working with ethics

Lynne Elvins
Naomi Goulder

Publisher's note

The subject of ethics is not new, yet its consideration within the applied visual arts is perhaps not as prevalent as it might be. Our aim here is to help a new generation of students, educators and practitioners find a methodology for structuring their thoughts and reflections in this vital area.

AVA Publishing hopes that these **Working with ethics** pages provide a platform for consideration and a flexible method for incorporating ethical concerns in the work of educators, students and professionals. Our approach consists of four parts:

The **introduction** is intended to be an accessible snapshot of the ethical landscape, both in terms of historical development and current dominant themes.

The **framework** positions ethical consideration into four areas and poses questions about the practical implications that might occur. Marking your response to each of these questions on the scale shown will allow your reactions to be further explored by comparison.

The **case study** sets out a real project and then poses some ethical questions for further consideration. This is a focus point for a debate rather than a critical analysis so there are no predetermined right or wrong answers.

A selection of **further reading** for you to consider areas of particular interest in more detail.

Ethical: awareness/ reflection/ debate

Working with ethics

Introduction

Ethics is a complex subject that interlaces the idea of responsibilities to society with a wide range of considerations relevant to the character and happiness of the individual. It concerns virtues of compassion, loyalty and strength, but also of confidence, imagination, humour and optimism. As introduced in ancient Greek philosophy, the fundamental ethical question is: *what should I do?* How we might pursue a 'good' life not only raises moral concerns about the effects of our actions on others, but also personal concerns about our own integrity.

In modern times the most important and controversial questions in ethics have been the moral ones. With growing populations and improvements in mobility and communications, it is not surprising that considerations about how to structure our lives together on the planet should come to the forefront. For visual artists and communicators, it should be no surprise that these considerations will enter into the creative process.

Some ethical considerations are already enshrined in government laws and regulations or in professional codes of conduct. For example, plagiarism and breaches of confidentiality can be punishable offences. Legislation in various nations makes it unlawful to exclude people with disabilities from accessing information or spaces. The trade of ivory as a material has been banned in many countries. In these cases, a clear line has been drawn under what is unacceptable.

But most ethical matters remain open to debate, among experts and lay-people alike, and in the end we have to make our own choices on the basis of our own guiding principles or values. Is it more ethical to work for a charity than for a commercial company? Is it unethical to create something that others find ugly or offensive?

Specific questions such as these may lead to other questions that are more abstract. For example, is it only effects on humans (and what they care about) that are important, or might effects on the natural world require attention too?

Is promoting ethical consequences justified even when it requires ethical sacrifices along the way? Must there be a single unifying theory of ethics (such as the Utilitarian thesis that the right course of action is always the one that leads to the greatest happiness of the greatest number), or might there always be many different ethical values that pull a person in various directions?

As we enter into ethical debate and engage with these dilemmas on a personal and professional level, we may change our views or change our view of others. The real test though is whether, as we reflect on these matters, we change the way we act as well as the way we think. Socrates, the 'father' of philosophy, proposed that people will naturally do 'good' if they know what is right. But this point might only lead us to yet another question: *how do we know what is right?*

You
What are your ethical beliefs?

Central to everything you do will be your attitude to people and issues around you. For some people, their ethics are an active part of the decisions they make every day as a consumer, a voter or a working professional. Others may think about ethics very little and yet this does not automatically make them unethical. Personal beliefs, lifestyle, politics, nationality, religion, gender, class or education can all influence your ethical viewpoint.

Using the scale, where would you place yourself? What do you take into account to make your decision? Compare results with your friends or colleagues.

Your client
What are your terms?

Working relationships are central to whether ethics can be embedded into a project, and your conduct on a day-to-day basis is a demonstration of your professional ethics. The decision with the biggest impact is whom you choose to work with in the first place. Cigarette companies or arms traders are often-cited examples when talking about where a line might be drawn, but rarely are real situations so extreme. At what point might you turn down a project on ethical grounds and how much does the reality of having to earn a living affect your ability to choose?

Using the scale, where would you place a project? How does this compare to your personal ethical level?

Your specifications
What are the impacts of your materials?

In relatively recent times, we are learning that many natural materials are in short supply. At the same time, we are increasingly aware that some man-made materials can have harmful, long-term effects on people or the planet. How much do you know about the materials that you use? Do you know where they come from, how far they travel and under what conditions they are obtained? When your creation is no longer needed, will it be easy and safe to recycle? Will it disappear without a trace? Are these considerations your responsibility or are they out of your hands?

Using the scale, mark how ethical your material choices are.

Your creation
What is the purpose of your work?

Between you, your colleagues and an agreed brief, what will your creation achieve? What purpose will it have in society and will it make a positive contribution? Should your work result in more than commercial success or industry awards? Might your creation help save lives, educate, protect or inspire? Form and function are two established aspects of judging a creation, but there is little consensus on the obligations of visual artists and communicators toward society, or the role they might have in solving social or environmental problems. If you want recognition for being the creator, how responsible are you for what you create and where might that responsibility end?

Using the scale, mark how ethical the purpose of your work is.

01 02 03 04 05 06 07 08 09 10

One aspect of fashion design that raises an ethical dilemma is the way that clothes production has changed in terms of the speed of delivery of products and the now international chain of suppliers. 'Fast fashion' gives shoppers the latest styles sometimes just weeks after they first appeared on the catwalk, at prices that mean they can wear an outfit once or twice and then replace it. Due to lower labour costs in poorer countries, the vast majority of Western clothes are made in Asia, Africa, South America or Eastern Europe in potentially hostile and sometimes inhumane working conditions. It can be common for one piece of clothing to be made up of components from five or more countries, often thousands of miles apart, before they end up in the high-street store. How much responsibility should a fashion designer have in this situation if manufacture is controlled by retailers and demand is driven by consumers? Even if designers wish to minimise the social impact of fashion, what might they most usefully do?

Traditional Hawaiian feather capes (called *'Ahu'ula*) were made from thousands of tiny bird feathers and were an essential part of aristocratic regalia. Initially they were red (*'Ahu'ula* literally means 'red garment') but yellow feathers, being especially rare, became more highly prized and were introduced to the patterning.

The significance of the patterns, as well as their exact age or place of manufacture is largely unknown, despite great interest in their provenance in more recent times. Hawaii was visited in 1778 by English explorer Captain James Cook and feather capes were amongst the objects taken back to Britain.

The basic patterns are thought to reflect gods or ancestral spirits, family connections and an individual's rank or position in society. The base layer for these garments is a fibre net, with the surface made up of bundles of feathers tied to the net in overlapping rows. Red feathers came from the *'i'iwi* or the *'apapane*. Yellow feathers came from a black bird with yellow tufts under each wing called *'oo'oo*, or a *mamo* with yellow feathers above and below the tail.

Thousands of feathers were used to make a single cape for a high chief (the feather cape of King Kamehameha the Great is said to have been made from the feathers of around 80,000 birds). Only the highest-ranking chiefs had the resources to acquire enough feathers for a full-length cape, whereas most chiefs wore shorter ones which came to the elbow.

The demand for these feathers was so great that they acquired commercial value and provided a full-time job for professional feather-hunters. These fowlers studied the birds and caught them with nets or with bird lime smeared on branches. As both the *'i'iwi* and *'apapane* were covered with red feathers, the birds were killed and skinned. Other birds were captured at the beginning of the moulting season, when the yellow display feathers were loose and easily removed without damaging the birds.

The royal family of Hawaii eventually abandoned the feather cape as the regalia of rank in favour of military and naval uniforms decorated with braid and gold. The *'oo'oo* and the *mamo* became extinct through the destruction of their forest feeding grounds and imported bird diseases. Silver and gold replaced red and yellow feathers as traded currency and the manufacture of feather capes became a largely forgotten art.

Is it more ethical to create clothing for the masses rather than for a few high-ranking individuals?

Is it unethical to kill animals to make garments?

Would you design and make a feather cape?

Fashion is a form of ugliness so intolerable that we have to alter it every six months.

Oscar Wilde

Further reading

AIGA
Design Business and Ethics
2007, AIGA

Eaton, Marcia Muelder
Aesthetics and the Good Life
1989, Associated University Press

Ellison, David
Ethics and Aesthetics in European Modernist Literature: From the Sublime to the Uncanny
2001, Cambridge University Press

Fenner, David E W (Ed)
Ethics and the Arts: An Anthology
1995, Garland Reference Library of Social Science

Gini, Al and Marcoux, Alexei M
Case Studies in Business Ethics
2005, Prentice Hall

McDonough, William and Braungart, Michael
Cradle to Cradle: Remaking the Way We Make Things
2002, North Point Press

Papanek, Victor
Design for the Real World: Making to Measure
1972, Thames & Hudson

United Nations Global Compact
The Ten Principles
www.unglobalcompact.org/AboutTheGC/TheTenPrinciples/index.html